A really useful guide to the
Tudors

KING HENRY
the SEVENTH

MARGARET
C^s of RICHMOND

IOHN EARL
of SOMERSET

JOHN DVKE
of LANCASTER

KING EDWARD
THE THIRD

Contents

Really useful family tree

Left: Henry VII by an unkno
Netherlandish artist, 1505

Centre right: Henry VIII by
Lucas Horenbout, c1526-7

Right: James I, after a portr
by John de Critz, (c1552-16

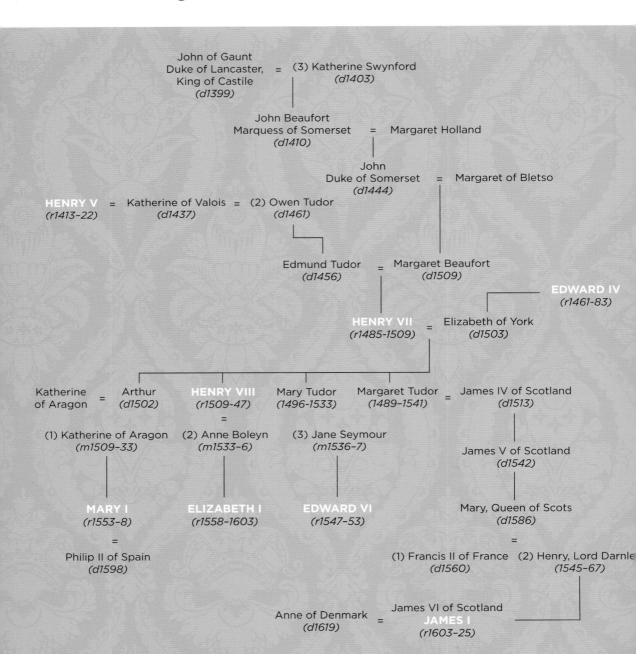

John of Gaunt
Duke of Lancaster,
King of Castile
(d1399)
= (3) Katherine Swynford
(d1403)

John Beaufort
Marquess of Somerset
(d1410)
= Margaret Holland

John
Duke of Somerset
(d1444)
= Margaret of Bletso

HENRY V
(r1413–22)
= Katherine of Valois
(d1437)
= (2) Owen Tudor
(d1461)

Edmund Tudor
(d1456)
= Margaret Beaufort
(d1509)

EDWARD IV
(r1461-83)

HENRY VII
(r1485-1509)
= Elizabeth of York
(d1503)

Katherine
of Aragon
= Arthur
(d1502)

HENRY VIII
(r1509-47)

Mary Tudor
(1496-1533)

Margaret Tudor
(1489–1541)
= James IV of Scotland
(d1513)

=

(1) Katherine of Aragon
(m1509–33)

(2) Anne Boleyn
(m1533-6)

(3) Jane Seymour
(m1536-7)

James V of Scotland
(d1542)

MARY I
(r1553-8)

ELIZABETH I
(r1558-1603)

EDWARD VI
(r1547-53)

Mary, Queen of Scots
(d1586)

=

Philip II of Spain
(d1598)

=

(1) Francis II of France
(d1560)

(2) Henry, Lord Darnle
(1545-67)

Anne of Denmark
(d1619)
=
James VI of Scotland
JAMES I
(r1603-25)

The Family of Henry VIII: An Allegory of the Tudor Succession by Lucas de Heere, c1570-75. Commissioned by Elizabeth I, it depicts (from left) Philip II of Spain, her half-sister Mary I, Henry VIII and her half brother Edward VI. Elizabeth herself holds the hand of 'Peace' signifying one of the attributes of her reign

Who were the Tudors?

The dynasty that never should have been

The Tudors – a family name that bears all the grandeur of royalty and power. Yet they should never have had a rightful claim to the throne of England, as they were descended from an illegitimate branch of the mighty House of Lancaster. The Lancaster families were to fight their rivals the House of York in the course of the 15th-century dynastic wars.

Coming up roses The royal line originated in John Beaufort, son of John of Gaunt, 1st Duke of Lancaster and third son of Edward III, and his mistress Katherine Swynford. Beaufort was made Earl of Somerset, and his illegitimacy was reversed by papal approval after his parents married.

Beaufort's grand-daughter Margaret married Edmund Tudor, 1st Earl of Richmond and the half-brother of the deranged and unhappy young king Henry VI. Owen Tudor, Edmund's father, had secretly married Queen Catherine of Valois, widow of Henry V, whose bodyguard he had been. The Tudors became passionate supporters of the Lancastrian cause, and were especially powerful in their father's native Wales.

Henry Tudor In January 1457, two months after Edmund had died, 14-year-old Margaret gave birth to a son at Pembroke Castle. The young Henry Tudor became the focus of hopes for the Lancaster cause against the dominant Yorkists, especially after the murder of Henry VI in 1471. Spirited away to France, there he sharpened his skills and developed his cause. Finally, after the death of Edward IV in 1483 and the disappearance of Edward V and his brother, supplanted by Richard III, the forces of discontent propelled Henry and his uncle Jasper Tudor into action.

Tudor family tree showing Henry VII, Henry VIII and his three children, from the 1596 Book of Statutes of the Plaisterers' Company

Bosworth Field Their invasion force landed at Milford Haven, and in the last great battle of the Wars of the Roses at Bosworth Field, Leicestershire on 22 August 1485, Henry Tudor defeated Richard of York. Legend has it that the crown had rolled from the head of Richard under a hawthorn bush when he was mercilessly killed, and it was extricated and placed on the victor's head on the battlefield. Richard was buried at Leicester Abbey, and his remains (discovered beneath a car park) were identified only in 2014.

Henry VII was proclaimed, a king against all the odds, and Tudor rule began.

Stained glass at Hampton Court Palace, showing the iconic Tudor rose. The badge combines the red rose of the House of Lancaster and the white of the House of York

Henry VII
1485-1509

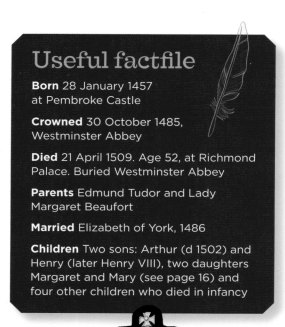

The victor at Bosworth who brought peace and stability One of the new king's first acts was to marry his third cousin Elizabeth of York, daughter of Edward IV and sister to Edward V. With this union, the once-warring houses were united, although that did not stop a series of plots and rebellions to overthrow Henry in favour of pretenders, Lambert Simnel in 1487 and Perkin Warbeck in 1490. They claimed to be the Earl of Warwick and the younger Prince in the Tower supposed to have been done away with by Richard III.

Security the watchword Not only did Henry VII have the security of his realm to establish, but he also had a dynasty to establish. England was a minor nation on the Atlantic fringe of Europe, no match for the other great powers. Yet through canny marriages, assisted by the treasure Henry amassed through aggressive revenue gathering, England entered a series of alliances. Arthur, Henry's elder son, was married to the Spanish princess Catherine of Aragon, a match that was a great coup. When Arthur died soon after, his next brother Henry was conveniently available to marry the young widow. Their sisters Margaret and Mary were married to the kings of Scotland and France respectively.

Mean man Henry VII was said to be careful and mean. Certainly he scrutinised the accounts, he pursued revenue from all quarters, and a vindictive streak ran through him. The warring chaos of the 15th century had been made worse by the rise of 'over-mighty subjects', territorial lords who raised private armies and demanded extreme loyalty from their own tenants and dependents. Henry VII's policy was clear: no man would have a lord other than him, and the once mighty lords were to be reduced in power.

The Tudor rose Henry's outward symbols of supreme power were badges, the heraldic symbols on clothes, buildings, horses and shields that showed allegiance. Now only the King's badges were to be allowed. The greatest of these came into its own when Henry died, the Tudor rose that incorporates the red and white roses of Lancaster and York, and was embodied in Henry VIII, the son of that union.

Emblem showing the Welsh dragon for Henry Tudor, in stained glass at Hampton Court Palace

Henry VII, attributed
to British School,
16th century

Palace connections

Henry VII used the **Tower of London** extensively. He held feasts and tournaments there to celebrate his victory over Richard III and also built more comfortable lodgings for himself and his family.

Henry VIII
1509-47

A mass of contradictions: 'golden' youth turned bloated bully, a loving man capable of shocking cruelty

Bust of a boy thought to be the young Henry, by Guido Mazzoni, c1498

Appearance The King is instantly recognisable to us as an older, overweight man. However, at 24 Henry was described as 'a golden prince'. He was unusually tall at 1.87m (6ft 2in), athletic, a graceful dancer and an indefatigable horseman. A serious jousting accident in 1536 left him with a leg injury that wouldn't heal, and he found it hard to exercise, although he still feasted, so his metabolism slowed. By 50 he was bloated (his waist measured 144cm/57in), his once shapely legs were ulcerated and he needed a wheelchair (Henry's 'tramme') to get around.

Personality Volatile, particularly as he grew older and less healthy. Henry was prone to quick-fire likes and dislikes. Some have described him as a spoilt child with a toy, who broke each person he had once loved into pieces when he had grown tired of them. In 1535 he reportedly nearly murdered a favourite fool for speaking well of his estranged wife, Katherine of Aragon, in his presence.

Second son syndrome Henry's elder brother Arthur had been due to inherit, but his premature death catapulted Henry into the position of heir to the throne. He had not been trained from birth, rather now his life changed. As the new and doubly precious heir, Henry was kept under strict supervision, away from the court for his own protection. This seclusion meant that in many ways he was unprepared to rule.

Brush with death A serious fall when jousting in 1536 left him unconscious for two hours. The shock is said to have caused Anne Boleyn to miscarry – she had been expecting a son. Some say the accident was a turning point, altering the King's personality and metabolism so that he grew monstrously fat. His leg injury never healed completely; the constant pain not helping his vicious temper and seemingly capricious cruelty in the latter part of his reign.

Henry VIII, after Hans Holbein the Younger, 153

Palace connections

Hampton Court Palace was Henry's 'pleasure palace', which he turned into a fabulous centre of entertainment, feasting, jousting and hunting. Henry married his sixth wife, Kateryn Parr at Hampton Court. His son Edward was born at the palace in 1537; 12 days later his mother Jane Seymour died there from birth complications. Henry imprisoned two of his wives, Anne Boleyn and Catherine Howard in the **Tower of London**. Both were executed on Tower Green.

Likes Henry was sports-mad, with a passion for hunting, hawking, jousting, swordplay, tennis and other activities of pleasure and exertion. For many years, before his 1536 accident, he was one of the best jousters in England. He could hunt all day as a young man; in later years he avoided an arduous chase by having the stags driven towards him so he could pick them off one by one. In one day's hunt in 1541 he and his courtiers shot 200 deer. He also loved music and dancing, and a number of songs and instrumental compositions are credited to him.

Illustration from the *Book of Simple Medicines*, c1470

The King resplendent in Victorian stained glass, in the Great Hall, Hampton Court Palace

Recreation of Henry's magnificent Crown of State, on display at Hampton Court Palace

Henry the hypochondriac The King was concerned with his health, maybe as a result of losing his parents early, and having only one male heir. He was a keen amateur apothecary and devised numerous healing remedies intended to ease the pain and inflammation of the legs that he suffered in later life. It is also thought that he suffered from gout, dropsy, and chronic sinusitis. He had a morbid fear of plague and sweating sickness, even abandoning his true love Anne Boleyn when she came down with a bout.

'The best dressed sovereign in the world' This was how Henry was once described by the admiring Venetian ambassador, who noted that the King had spent '16,000 ducats on the wardrobe'. Henry's outfits were sumptuous. He ordered a total of 79 during his reign; one made in 1537 was 'crimson velvet embroidered all over with damask gold and pearls and stones'. When it came to his bonnets he didn't spare the bling: one of his favourites was black velvet garnished with eight great rubies, diamonds and pearls. His nightshirts were silk; he had lots of shoes, slippers and even had shoes made to play Tudor-style football.

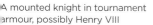

A mounted knight in tournament armour, possibly Henry VIII

Henry playing the harp, from the *Psalter of Henry VIII*, 1540

Henry as musician The King was a talented composer and musician, who liked music as background to court life. On occasion his personal organist Dennis Memmo, a favourite of Henry's, would play for over four hours at a stretch. By 1547 Henry had 60 musicians on his payroll, as well as choristers: The Gentlemen and Children of the Chapel Royal. The King nurtured talent for his choir as carefully as a football manager. Once, after a competition between their two chapel choirs, which Wolsey's won, Henry poached the best singers from the Cardinal's choir.

Henry the prankster The King loved disguise, and everyone had to pretend they didn't recognize the tall, burly monarch until he unmasked himself! As a young man he often played tricks on Cardinal Wolsey, on one occasion bursting into the Presence Chamber with a group of masked men, while the Cardinal had to play along. An older Henry also tried this trick on poor Anne of Cleves (see page 24). While en route to meet her husband–to–be, she was disturbed in her private rooms by a group of masked men. When the big guy with the beard tried to kiss her she pushed him away in disgust – which didn't go down well with Henry.

Sexual prowess Henry was certainly driven by lust, frustration and desire, but despite his reputation for womanising we only know of three definite mistresses. Elizabeth (Bessie) Blount, a great beauty, was a maid to Queen Katherine of Aragon. Henry also had a brief affair with Mary Boleyn, sister to Anne, during the 1520s. While Anne was still queen, a 'Mrs Shelton', Anne's first cousin, became his mistress for about six months before Jane Seymour caught his eye. Elizabeth Howard, Anne and Mary's mother, was also rumoured to have had a fling with Henry – who denied it, protesting, 'Never with the mother'!

A nightmarish Henry VIII, after Cornelis Matsys, 1744

What kind of ruler?

Henry VIII's reign was, arguably, the single most important in English history. The break with Rome (see page 34) made England a Protestant nation and the Dissolution of the Monasteries (see page 38) changed irreversibly the shape of land ownership and power. Parliament acquired greater authority than it had ever had before, and effective government was instituted throughout the country. Henry VIII helped make England into a European power. All this was played against the background of his six marriages and desperate race for an heir, which drove a good many of his actions and decisions.

A romantic vision of Henry's family life in *The Royal Nursery, 1538* by Marcus Stone (1840-1921)

A good father? Henry was, by many accounts an attentive and loving father. His two daughters as well as his son were very well taught and were brought up to be scholarly and accomplished. He indulged his illegitimate son Henry Fitzroy, treating him generously and making him Duke of Richmond. Nothing was too grand for his true heir, Prince Edward, of course. The little prince even had his own fighting bears. Mary and Elizabeth were loved, ostracised and reconciled in their turn as a reaction to the fates of their mothers.

Henry's wider family

Arthur
1486-1502

As second son, Henry never expected to become king. His elder brother Arthur married Katherine of Aragon, and then died of consumption at the age of 15. Life changed dramatically for Henry, as his carefree life of a playboy prince came to an end.

Arthur, Prince of Wales, British School, c1520

Margaret, Queen of Scots
1489-1541

Henry's elder sister Margaret was married by proxy at the age of 13 to James IV, King of Scotland in 1502. She did her duty by becoming mother of an heir, the future James V of Scotland

Mary, Queen of France
1496-1533

Mary Tudor, Henry's younger sister, was thought to be one of the most beautiful women in the world, but was married off, in 1541, to Louis XII of France, gouty, toothless and ancient. Luckily for her he died after only a few months, leaving her free to marry her sweetheart, handsome Charles Brandon, Duke of Suffolk.

Henry Fitzroy
1539-36

Bessie Blount, an early mistress of Henry's, gave him a son, Henry Fitzroy in 1519. Henry rewarded her well and treated young Henry handsomely, giving him a household of his own. In the absence of a legitimate son, Henry was the King's designated heir for a while But he died just before Edward was born.

Henry Fitzroy, Duke of Richmo and Somerset, c1533-4

Mary, Queen of Scots and her son James VI (James I of England), by an unknown artist, 1583. In reality, the Queen never saw her son after her abdication and imprisionment in 1567

Lady Jane Grey

1537-54

Henry's sister Mary and Charles Brandon had a son, Henry. His eldest daughter Jane, a strong Protestant was proposed as a rival queen to Catholic Mary when Edward VI died. Forced to take the throne, she reigned for nine days before Mary's I's forces deposed her, and she was executed at the Tower. (See also page 48.)

Mary, Queen of Scots

1542-87

Henry's nephew James V produced a daughter, Mary Stuart, later Queen of Scots. She married the Dauphin, heir of the French throne, and spent time in France. When Mary I of England died, Mary Stuart's Tudor blood made her a viable

Catholic alternative to the Protestant Queen Elizabeth. Her second husband, Lord Darnley, was murdered in 1564 and she was forced to abdicate. Elizabeth I eventually had the fugitive Mary, Queen of Scots locked up, and at length she was executed at Fotheringhay Castle on 8 February 1587 (see also page 66). Mary left a son, who became James VI of Scotland and then James I of England when he succeeded in 1603.

James VI of Scotland and I of England

1566-1625

When Elizabeth I died childless in 1603, it meant that Henry VIII's Tudor dynasty petered out. So the Stuarts of Scotland were invited to take Elizabeth's place, which is why James is the sixth king of that name in Scotland but the first in England.

Katherine of Aragon

Married 1509-33

An extremely pious, gentle-seeming girl, with a steely determination that emerged in later life.

Useful factfile

Born 16 December 1485, near Madrid, Spain

Parents Isabella of Castille and Ferdinand of Aragon

Married (1) Arthur, 1501 (died 2 April 1502), (2) Henry VIII, 11 June 1509, both at Westminster Abbey

Ages at marriage She was 23, Henry was 17

Children At least five stillbirths, numerous miscarriages, a son who lived for only a couple of months; surviving daughter, Princess Mary (*b*18 February 1516), later Mary I

Marriage annulled 23 May 1533 (never accepted by Katherine)

Died 7 January 1536, aged 50, in exile at Buckden, Huntingdonshire. Likely cause of death was stomach cancer. Buried Peterborough Abbey

Katherine became stubborn to the point of self-destruction

Why her? By marrying Katherine, his brother's widow, Henry continued the useful political alliance with her powerful parents. Isabella and Ferdinand were an astonishing couple with huge influence in Europe and beyond. And by all accounts, Henry loved her.

Appearance Fair skinned, with reddish-gold hair and an oval face and sweet demeanour. However, she was very short, and multiple pregnancies left her dumpy.

Finest hour Katherine was left in charge of the country in 1513 when Henry went to war against France. He trusted her with the Regency and the defence of the realm against France's ally, Scotland.

Greatest tragedy Not producing a son for Henry, after at least eight stillbirths or miscarriages.

Well-matched Despite the unusual circumstances of their marriage, and the fact that Catherine was 6 years older than Henry, they were loving partners. They shared an education and piety (although Katherine was more intense), loved finery and display, rode and hunted together. They were married, mainly happily, for over 20 years.

Personal style Katherine was outwardly serene while her husband was youthfully exuberant; as a younger woman she tolerated his sometimes childish pranks. Later in their marriage, she tried to hide her frustration and hurt at his increasing infidelity. Her stoicism finally broke under a sense of huge injustice and religious outrage when he sought to have their marriage annulled.

Worst mistake Not going quietly. By acknowledging the inevitable Katherine could have left court and lived out her days peacefully and comfortably. She became stubborn to the point of self-destruction. Even her daughter was taken from her and she died without seeing Mary again.

Unhappy end: Henry became convinced that God was punishing him for marrying his brother's widow. Katherine denied that her first marriage had been consummated, and therefore no sin had been committed, but Henry already had Anne Boleyn in his dreams and the Pope in his sights. After a long and messy annulment trial Katherine was dismissed from court.

Katherine of Aragon, Anglo-Flemish School, c1530

Henry's wives
Anne Boleyn

Married 1533, executed 1536

Spirited, witty and egged on by
ambitious relatives to woo the King.

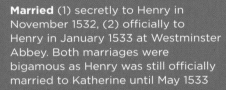

Useful factfile

Born around 1501

Married (1) secretly to Henry in
November 1532, (2) officially to
Henry in January 1533 at Westminster
Abbey. Both marriages were
bigamous as Henry was still officially
married to Katherine until May 1533

Ages at marriage She was 31-2,
he was 41

Children One daughter Elizabeth, later
Elizabeth I, born 7 September 1533.
Anne also suffered several
miscarriages and a stillbirth

Died Tower of London, 19 May 1536,
executed for adultery, incest and
high treason. Buried in the Chapel of
St Peter ad Vincula, Tower of London

Parents Sir Thomas Boleyn and
Lady Elizabeth Howard

Tall, striking, dark, exuding glamour, style and sex appeal

Why her? Henry was tiring of his ageing first wife, who had failed to provide him with a surviving male heir, when he first spied Anne, Katherine's lady-in-waiting, in 1526. Anne had been educated in France, and she was a glamorous addition to Henry's court, with French-learnt manners and etiquette, a skilful player of the flirting game of 'courtly love'. With the King this comparatively harmless pastime among courtiers soon turned into a serious affair. Her conniving relatives urged her to aim for the highest prize. It seems Anne refused to consummate the relationship unless Henry made her his queen. Passionately determined to have her, Henry set about the momentous events that led to the end of his marriage to Katherine and the 'break with Rome'

Appearance Tall, striking, dark, exuding glamour, style and sex appeal. Her French fashions set her apart. Poised and elegant, particularly good at dancing, which she had learnt at the French court as lady-in-waiting to her sister Mary (who had previously been Henry's mistress).

Wry sense of humour On the day of her execution, she comforted herself by saying 'I heard say the executioner was very good, and I have a little neck', before laughing heartily (or possibly hysterically).

Worst insults Anne wasn't popular in the country as a whole, as most people sympathised with Henry's first wife Katherine. Wolsey resented her influence on the King and called her 'the night crow' – cawing into Henry's ear as they lay together. In 1535 a Margaret Chandelier of Suffolk confessed before justices that she had called the Queen a 'goggle-eyed whore'.

Unhappy end Henry ordered Anne's execution after she was accused and found guilty on trumped up charges of adultery, incest and high treason. This took place at the Tower of London on 19 May 1536. The King showed her a small 'mercy' at the end. As she had requested, Anne was beheaded cleanly with a sword, not an axe, as was the French custom.

A BOLINA VXOR— HENRI· OCTA

Copy of a presumed lost
portrait of Anne Boleyn,
by an unknown artist,
c1533-36

Henry's wives
Jane Seymour

Married 1536, died 1537

Dowdy, but she delivered. Henry's favourite queen gave him the son he longed for.

Useful factfile

Born around 1509

Married May 1536

Ages at marriage she was 26-27, he was 44

Children Prince Edward, later Edward VI, born at Hampton Court 12 October 1537

Died 24 October 1537 at Hampton Court, of post-natal complications. Buried St George's Chapel, Windsor

Parents Sir John Seymour and Margery Wentworth

Why her? Anne Boleyn had given Henry a healthy daughter, but no son. And the King was tiring of Anne's temper; their flaming rows and passionate making-up had been stimulating in a mistress, but were tedious in a wife. Jane, a lady-in-waiting, was quiet, seemingly unambitious, demure, and a calming presence. Henry apparently wrote to her while he was still married to Anne Boleyn. In one letter he described himself as Jane's 'entirely devoted servant ... hoping short to receive you in these arms'. They were married just 11 days after Anne's execution.

Appearance Nothing special: the Spanish ambassador described her 'of middling stature and no great beauty'. He even speculated that it was her prowess in bed that had attracted Henry!

Great gifts Henry showered Jane with jewellery and gifts during their courtship and brief marriage. A list of her jewels survives and designs for the most elaborate – with Henry and Jane's initials entwined – may be seen at the British Museum. Hans Holbein, who painted Jane during her lifetime, also designed a very beautiful gem-studded cup that Henry gave to his favourite queen.

Victim or schemer? Jane's family were the ambitious, scheming Seymours. Noble but obscure, they were pulled into the limelight when Jane married Henry, and their ambition knew no bounds. Two of her brothers were later executed for treason. Jane's own reputation has fluctuated over the years from 'innocent victim of Henry's dynastic quest' and 'powerless to resist the King's advances' to a ruthless schemer who encouraged him. The truth is probably somewhere in the middle.

Unhappy end Jane developed what were probably post-natal complications after the difficult birth, and although she was present to witness part of Edward's magnificent christening held at Hampton Court her condition worsened. She died nearly two weeks after the birth, aged only 28, and Henry was reportedly heartbroken.

The good die young By dying at the height of her 'success', delivering Henry his longed-for heir and before he had a chance to tire of her, Jane left an indelible impression of perfection. Of all his queens, Henry chose to be buried next to her in St George's Chapel, Windsor.

Jane Seymour, by Hans Holbein the Younger, c1536

Jane was
seemingly
unambitious,
demure, and
a calming
presence

23

Anne of Cleves

Married January 1540, divorced July 1540

A political rather than romantic union, but their marriage was doomed from the start.

Useful factfile

Born 15 September 1515

Married 6 January 1540, at the Queen's Closet, Greenwich Palace

Ages at marriage She was 24, he was 48

Marriage annulled July 1540

Children none

Died 16 July 1557 at Chelsea Manor. Buried Westminster Abbey

Parents John III Duke of Cleves and Maria of Jülich-Berg

Why her? Marrying Anne was a political move to bring Henry support in Europe. He also knew that it would be wise to have a 'spare' to add to his heir. A marriage with the German Duchy of Cleves seemed to offer the best alliance. Anne and her younger sister Amelia were both painted by Holbein and dangled as bait. Henry chose Anne as more mature (she was all of 24 compared to Amelia's 22) and so more suitable for a man in his late 40s.

Appearance Not as bad as legend has it. It became fashionable to criticise her looks, her clothes, her manners and her personal hygiene over the years and she only became known as the 'Flanders Mare' in the 17th century.

Fact or fiction? This portrait of Anne by Holbein has been said to have idealised her for Henry's eyes so that he agreed to marriage, only to be disgusted by the real Anne. However, this probably isn't true. The political motivation for marrying Anne had receded by the time she got to England, and Henry began to look for excuses to get out of his obligation.

Most embarrassing moment While en route from Rochester to London, Anne was surprised in her chambers by a group of masked and cloaked men, led by a tall, burly middle-aged man who tried to kiss her. Anne, bewildered and unprepared, pushed him away. Henry, who had led the foray himself, was devastated by her lack of wit and panache. 'I like her not' he declared on his way back to Greenwich.

Wedding nightmare Despite Thomas Cromwell's desperate attempt to find a respectable loophole, the wedding went ahead, and the Anglo-Cleves agreement was sealed on Twelfth Night 1540 in a tense ceremony. The wedding night was even worse. Anne's total innocence and Henry's impatience and intermittent impotence were a disastrous combination. After persisting for four nights, Henry gave up, blaming his failure to consummate the marriage on Anne's physical repulsiveness.

Happy end The marriage was annulled six months later. Anne and Henry remained on friendly terms and she was rewarded for her acquiescence with a generous grant of land worth £3000 a year. Anne lived out her days surrounded by German servants at Hever Castle, which she turned into a miniature Rhenish court.

Anne of Cleves,
by Hans Holbein
the Younger, 1539

Catherine Howard

Married 1540, executed 1542

Flirtatious teenager who captured Henry's heart, but her infidelity spurred him to vicious revenge.

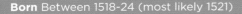

Useful factfile

Born Between 1518-24 (most likely 1521)

Married 28 July 1540 at Oatlands Palace

Ages at marriage She was 17-22, he was 49

Children none

Died Executed at the Tower of London for adultery, 13 February 1542. Buried St Peter ad Vincula

Parents Lord Edmund Howard (younger brother of the Duke of Norfolk) and Joyce Culpeper

Why her? Henry, fresh from his disappointing – and unconsummated – marriage to Anne of Cleves, had probably already spotted vivacious young Catherine among Anne's ladies-in-waiting. This time he wanted to marry for love, and although keenly aware of his increasing age and corpulence, he wanted her. Catherine, an experienced flirt, soon had the King besotted, and the Howard family were quick to encourage their young charge. Henry could barely keep his hands off her in public.

Early life Catherine's parents both died young, so she was brought up in the enormous household of her step-grandmother the Dowager Duchess of Norfolk. While giving her the conventional training of a young aristocrat, the Dowager Duchess was a careless chaperone. The maids' quarters in the rambling mansion in Horsham were unsupervised, and Catherine and her young female friends were able to entertain admirers freely, in an age when an upper-class girl's 'honour' was her most vital asset.

Early loves Catherine had her first romantic liaison aged 14 with a young music teacher, Henry Manox, although she later swore that they had not had sex. She had a more serious, sexually active relationship with a young noble, Francis Dereham, between 1537 and 1539.

Worst mistake Thinking she could continue her sexual liaisons after marriage, too. It seems likely that she entertained a Gentleman of the King's Privy Chamber, Thomas Culpeper, with the help of her maid, Jane Boleyn, Lady Rochford. The affair continued right under Henry's nose while the royal party were on royal progress in 1541.

Unhappy end Rumours finally reached the ear of the Archbishop of Canterbury, who had the unenviable task of telling the King while he was at prayer at Hampton Court on 2 November 1541. Henry shrugged it off as slander, but the arrests and confessions of her lovers under torture confirmed the worst. Henry ordered Catherine's arrest on 6 November and never saw her again. In February the terrified young woman was taken to the Tower of London by barge, passing under the rotting heads of Culpeper and Dereham displayed on London Bridge. Three days later she was beheaded, followed by her accomplice Lady Rochford.

Ghostly legacy It's said that Catherine's ghost haunts Hampton Court Palace, her screams for mercy echoing down what is known today as 'The Haunted Gallery'.

A 16th-century portrait of a young woman thought to be Catherine Howard by a follower of Hans Holbein the Younger

Inset: Catherine's ghostly legend lives on in this Victorian postcard

The Ghost, Hampton Court Palace

Kateryn loved
gorgeous fabrics
(crimson was her
favourite colour),
fine perfumes
and jewels

Kateryn Parr,
attributed to Master
John, c1545

Henry's wives
Kateryn Parr

Married 1543-7

Kind, patient and sensible woman, who provided love and stability to Henry's three children and comfort to the ageing King.

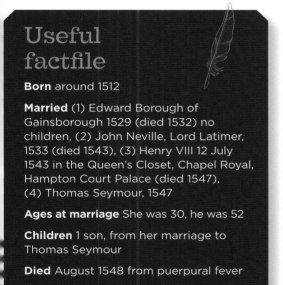

Useful factfile

Born around 1512

Married (1) Edward Borough of Gainsborough 1529 (died 1532) no children, (2) John Neville, Lord Latimer, 1533 (died 1543), (3) Henry VIII 12 July 1543 in the Queen's Closet, Chapel Royal, Hampton Court Palace (died 1547), (4) Thomas Seymour, 1547

Ages at marriage She was 30, he was 52

Children 1 son, from her marriage to Thomas Seymour

Died August 1548 from puerpural fever

Parents Sir Thomas Parr of Kendal and Maude Green

Why her? Kateryn met the King in the winter of 1542-3 when she became a lady in the household of Henry's daughter, Princess Mary. Henry was 52, corpulent and ill, probably looking for a stable, caring companion. Twice-widowed Kateryn Parr was 30, but in no way an old maid. She was in fact younger than Anne Boleyn when she married Henry a decade earlier.

Greatest strength Henry relied on Kateryn to run the country during his absence at war with France in 1544.

Greatest achievement Apart from being the only wife to survive Henry VIII, Kateryn was the first Queen of England to write and publish her own books and the first Englishwoman to publish a work of prose in the 16th century. She was also an active patron of the arts, supporting artists and artisans.

Worst mistake Although sensible and self-controlled in most things, Kateryn occasionally pushed her evangelical views too far with Henry when discussing religion. Her religious opponents seized on this and persuaded Henry that she could be dangerous. Plans were drawn up for her arrest, signed by Henry himself. Kateryn, forewarned of the peril she faced, was persuaded to throw herself on Henry's mercy and plead forgiveness. Henry was completely disarmed, and forgave her.

Pleasures Kateryn was fond of the simple things in life – animals, flowers, laughter – and she kept jesters both male and female. 'Mirth and modesty' are words used to describe her, but she wasn't dull and had a taste for luxury. Kateryn particularly loved gorgeous fabrics (crimson was her favourite colour), fine perfumes and jewels. Her privy wardrobe accounts even record that she bought a black silk nightgown!

Happy(ish) end With Henry dead, Kateryn was at last free to wed her sweetheart Thomas Seymour, whom she had given up to marry Henry, and was delighted soon to be pregnant. Sadly, Kateryn contracted puerpural fever just after the birth of a healthy son, and her handsome, much-loved husband was at her side when she died.

Henry's men behind the throne

Cardinal Thomas Wolsey
c1475-1530

Thomas Wolsey was a butcher's son who became the most dominant churchman and politician in the land. He gained great power and received glittering rewards for his service, having made himself indispensable to the pleasure-loving young Henry VIII. Wolsey not only ran the realm and serviced Henry's wars, he indulged the royal appetite for masques, banqueting and other entertainments. Wolsey turned the manor house of Hampton Court into a glittering palace in which to entertain the King, who for a long time regarded the older man with great affection. However, Wolsey's failure to deliver the King's deepest desire – a divorce – killed that affection. When news came that the Pope had categorically forbidden Henry's remarriage to Anne Boleyn, Wolsey was disgraced. In November 1530 he was arrested on his way back to London from Yorkshire and accused of treason, then fell ill and died in Leicester Abbey (now Abbey Park) on 29 November 1530.

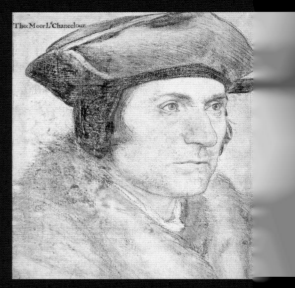

Sir Thomas More, by Hans Holbein the Younger, c1526-

Sir Thomas More
1478-1535

Lord Chancellor, scholar and humanist

With a background as a classical scholar an[d] More joined the king's council in 1517-8, and knighted in 1521. He served on overseas dele[gations] and became secretary to Cardinal Wolsey, b[efore] succeeding Wolsey to become Henry VIII's f[irst] minister in 1529, and Lord Chancellor. More'[s] principles were to be his undoing. He refuse[d to] swear an oath to the 1534 Act of Successio[n,] rejected papal supremacy and recognised H[enry] as supreme head of the Church of England. [He] was found guilty of treason in 1535 and alth[ough he] was sentenced to a traitor's death, Henry ha[d it] commuted to beheading.

Cardinal Wolsey, by an unknown artist, c1520

Thomas Cromwell
1485-1540

Earl of Essex, first minister

The son of a south London brewer-blacksmith, the clever, dynamic Cromwell so impressed Henry VIII that he made him the second most powerful man in England. Cromwell had first made his mark as legal adviser to Cardinal Wolsey, and was appointed as Henry's first minister in 1533. Henry knighted him three years later, which brought Cromwell a host of fancy titles and the power to work on the King's behalf to exercise Henry's newly established royal supremacy. But from these lofty heights he suddenly toppled – and in July 1540 was executed, shortly after having been created Earl of Essex. His fall is something of a mystery, possibly the work of his many enemies at court.

Thomas Cromwell, Earl of Essex, after Hans Holbein the Younger, 1532-3

Stephen Gardiner
c1495-1555

Bishop of Winchester

A protégé of Cardinal Wolsey's, Gardiner's legal and diplomatic skills brought him to Henry's attention. He was soon the King's principal secretary, working to secure his divorce from Katherine of Aragon. He was rewarded with the wealthy and important bishopric of Winchester, but his career took a downturn in the 1530s, when he was suspected of opposing Henry's religious policies. The fall of Thomas Cromwell (in which Gardiner probably had a hand) paved the way for his return to favour, and for the rest of the reign he was one of the leading figures at court, where he played a key role in foreign affairs and continued to resist radical religious change.

Stephen Gardiner, English School, 16th century

Thomas Cranmer
1489-1556

Archbishop of Canterbury

Academic cleric Cranmer found the legal and historical precedents to support Henry's break with Rome. Henry rewarded him by making him Archbishop in 1533. Cranmer helped shape the English Reformation. He had the unenviable task of telling the King of Catherine Howard's infidelities, but his simplicity, humility and wisdom kept Henry's favour, despite several plots against him in the 1540s.

Thomas Cranmer, by Gerlach Flicke, 1545-6

European ambitions

Henry as warrior and statesman Henry fancied himself as a Renaissance prince. He wanted to make a big noise in Europe, to be respected and feared. This was in complete contrast to his father who preferred to build up power through canny alliances and marriages. Around Henry VIII a new European order was emerging. France was increasingly hemmed in by the combined dynasties of the Habsburgs, who ruled Spain, Italy and the Holy Roman Empire (encompassing modern-day Germany and beyond). Henry was keen to make his mark and he struck an increasingly important figure.

Emperor Henry? The King even considered standing for election as the Holy Roman Emperor in 1519 (with Wolsey eyeing up the Pope's job alongside him), an totally unrealistic ambition that was thwarted in 1519 when Habsburg Emperor Charles V (nephew of Katherine of Aragon) was elected. Power went back and forth, allies were made and lost, and the whole period is characterised by this geopolitical game that was just beginning (and would continue for centuries).

> Francis I, King of France, was roughly Henry's age, handsome and accomplished. Henry saw him both as a personal and political rival

The Embarkation of Henry VIII at Dover, British School, c1520-40

The Field of Cloth of Gold, British School, c1545

Henry's rival Francis I, King of France, was roughly Henry's age, handsome and accomplished. Henry saw him both as a personal and political rival. France was struggling for dominance in Western Europe with the Habsburg Empire, and when the relationship Charles V soured, Henry tried to make up with France.

Francis I, by Francois Clouet, c1510-72

The Field of Cloth of Gold, 1520. This wildly extravagant diplomatic mission was a showpiece meeting between Henry and Francis, planned by Cardinal Wolsey. The meeting place covered an area of nearly 12,000 square yards, lavish arrangements were made for jousting, dancing and banqueting. (see Feasting page 86). The event earned its name for the dazzling quantity of gold cloth used, but didn't achieve England's ambitions and worse, proved humiliating for Henry. When the young, fit king challenged Francis to a wrestling match, the French king threw Henry to the floor. It must have also been galling that Francis's young and fertile queen was glowingly pregnant with one of their many heirs.

A costly mistake? After achieving little through expensive diplomacy, Henry switched tactics and allegiances, siding with the apparently successful Habsburgs, England declared war on France. This was a very costly war, paid for through increased taxation, which led to resentment at home. Eventually Henry and Wolsey abandoned the Habsburg Emperor Charles and signed a peace treaty with France. This proved another mistake, as this affected England's valuable trade in cloth with the Habsburg-controlled Netherlands. Worse still, it angered the Pope (who was under the thumb of the Emperor), so destroying Henry's chances of papal approval for his divorce from the Emperor's aunt, Katherine of Aragon.

The King's Great Matter – and the break from Rome

What was it? So all-consuming was Henry's desire to pursue the Pope to grant him a divorce from Katherine of Aragon that it became known as the King's 'Great Matter'. In the end Henry and his ministers were unsuccessful, so the King broke away from the Church of Rome and established himself head of the Church in England. No longer would he have to answer to any man on earth, including the Pope.

What caused it? Henry's first wife Katherine of Aragon, six years his senior, had only produced one healthy child (Princess Mary, in 1516), followed by a string of miscarriages and still births. As she reached her mid-thirties, Henry began to despair of having a male heir. What could he do?

Next! By 1536 the King was infatuated with one of Katherine's ladies-in-waiting, Anne Boleyn, which spurred him on to action. After pondering the scriptures, Henry announce that he had disobeyed the Bible in marrying Katherine, as it specifically forbade a man to marry his brother's widow. Aided and abetted by interpretation from his closest advisers, Henry tried to divorce Katherine on these grounds, claiming that he was being punished as God was denying him a male heir. Despite Katherine fighting back strongly, declaring that her marriage to Arthur had not been consummated, Henry had made up his mind.

The scapegoats All envoys to the Rome were rebuffed. Furious, and spurred on by his desire for Anne, Henry turned on Wolsey, blaming him for the failure, and charged his devoted minister with treason. Weakened and dispirited, the Cardinal fell. He died on his way back to London to stand trial for treason.

Thomas More tried to persuade Henry to have Katherine back. Henry wouldn't listen, and asserted that his position as king made him supreme in his own realm, so he owed obedience to no earthly power (the Pope). Thomas More was sent to the Tower and executed for failing to support Henry's plans (see also page 36). In January 1533 Henry wed Anne Boleyn. The new Archbishop of Canterbury, Thomas Cranmer declared Henry's marriage to Katherine null and void.

Detail of stained glass window depicting Henry VIII praying, from the Tudor chapel at The Vyne, Hampshire

Katherine of Aragon, by an unknown artist, early 18th century

Henry's reign
The Reformation

What was it? Henry had achieved the divorce he wanted when he took England out of the Roman Catholic Church and declared himself head of the English Church. He began to separate from Rome, a process speeded up when he was excommunicated by the Pope in retaliation. But for Henry 'reform' was about changing who held the power in the English Church, rather than doctrinal change, despite key figures around him having far more radical views.

Henry's own faith Henry was actually quite conservative in his beliefs. Back in 1521, he had written a book attacking arch-Reformist Luther, which had earned him the title 'Defender of the Faith' from the Pope. Henry had acted pragmatically in his split from Rome, but for the rest of his life he would be a Catholic, if not a Roman Catholic.

1534 Act of Supremacy A further step in the break with Rome came with this Act, drawn up by Henry's bright new minister and Wolsey's protégé, Thomas Cromwell. This act made 'the King's

Highness to be the Supreme Head of the Church of England and to have authority to reform and redress all error, heresies and abuses in the same'. Secular political authority replaced ecclesiastical power in creating the Church of England.

With the power play sorted, Henry was content to practise his watered-down Catholicism, but others around him, including Cromwell, Archbishop Cranmer and Anne Boleyn herself, had pro-Luther sympathies. Still others were strongly traditional, and refused to acknowledge Henry as supreme leader of the Church. When Sir Thomas More, who had replaced Wolsey, could not find it within his conscience to acknowledge Royal Supremacy, Henry had him imprisoned in the Tower and executed for treason in 1535.

A more cautious King Although Henry commissioned an English translation of the Bible (a key demand of Protestant reformers), the Act of Six Articles asserted a number of traditional Catholic doctrines, such as transubstantiation and celibacy for priests.

The Pilgrimage of Grace imagined in this 19th-century print

Right: The Pope suppressed by Henry VIII, from Foxe's *Book of Martyrs*, first published 1563, showing Pope Clement VII under the King's feet in 1534

Pilgrimage of Grace

There were reactions to Henry's religious policies in the wider country, too. In 1536, a serious rebellion broke out in the north of England, which interrupted the process of Dissolution of the Monasteries (see page 38). Although the uprising was brutally suppressed by use of martial law and public hangings it demonstrated weaknesses in the power of the state.

Dissolution of the Monasteries

1536-40

What was it? Although the monasteries were not an initial or necessary target in the Reformation process, they were an easy target. Stories of fat abbots, concubines, loose living and fleecing credulous pilgrims circulated widely. Henry had no particular doctrinal issue at stake; aided by his first minister Cromwell, he could see the riches of the monasteries and decided to help himself.

What took place? Under Thomas Cromwell, the first wave dissolving all religious houses of monks, canons and nuns with a value below £200 and where 'manifest sin, vicious carnal and abominable living is daily used and committed' began in 1536 and continued in a second wave from 1538 until 1541. Not all monasteries were hotbeds of sin; many provided charity, hospitality, education and spiritual welfare. The commissioners ruthlessly closed down over 800, destroying architectural and artistic treasures that had been at the centre of English culture for over a thousand years.

Metal pilgrim badges were souvenirs sold to those who made religious journeys to their favourite shrines

Right: Badge from Walsingham depicting the Virgin and the Angel Gabriel

Left and below: Badges from the shrine of Thomas Becket

Glastonbury Abbey with the Tor beyond, by George Arnald (1763-1841)

Lincolnshire rebelled against the closures and abbot Matthew Mackerel of Barings Abbey was accused of feeding and encouraging the rebels. Seizing the excuse, Cromwell had this rich monastery closed and Mackerel and six of his brethren were hanged. The most famous case of resistance was at Glastonbury. The wealth of this abbey was legendary, and abbot Richard Whiting resisted surrender, hiding money and treasure about the building away from the King's prying commissioners. But they swooped and found 'seditious books' in his study. Whiting was condemned, dragged to the top of Glastonbury Tor with two of his brethren, and hanged, drawn and quartered.

What was the end result? Most of the extensive monastic lands ended up in the hands of the aristocracy and a rising new class of country gentlemen. Some of the buildings were plundered for materials, such as Chertsey Abbey in Surrey, which provided material for the King's palaces at Hampton Court and Oatlands.

Edward VI

1547-53

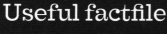

Useful factfile

Born 12 October 1537 at Hampton Court Palace

Crowned 20 February 1547, aged 9, Westminster Abbey

Died 6 July 1553, aged 15, Greenwich Palace. Buried Westminster Abbey

Parents Henry VIII and Jane Seymour

Married Never

Children; None

The hoped-for son and heir who never reached adulthood

The longed-for Prince Henry VIII wept for joy on first holding his baby son. 'England's treasure', he called him. The new prince was named Edward for Edward the Confessor, as he was born on 12 October, the eve of the royal saint's feast day. Here was the hoped-for son and heir, who would become a great king and continue the bloodline.

Joy and pain The child's baptism at Hampton Court three days later was a great state occasion. However, Queen Jane Seymour was absent, in her bed, dying from a massive haemorrhage caused by the placenta left inside her womb. She succumbed, and Henry mourned her ever after.

Prince Edward The boy grew to be bonny and strong, Hans Holbein painted him serene and holding his baby's rattle like a sceptre. Until he was 6 he was brought up among women; some rocked his cradle, a wet nurse breastfed him and a dry nurse changed him. She was Sibil Penn, wife of a groom of Henry's chamber; her ghost is still said to haunt Hampton Court Palace. The nursery, with Edward and his half-sister Elizabeth, moved from house to house, complete with a company of players to entertain the royal children.

Household and education Everything changed when Edward was 6. He caught malaria at Hampton Court; he first truly showed the stubborn streak he had inherited; and he began his formal and formidable education. Edward flourished in the household of Queen Kateryn Parr, his father's sixth and last wife, and he was given a set of tutors, all Cambridge-educated humanists and evangelical reformers. He was fluent in Latin, Greek and French before he was 8.

Below: Part of Edward's christening procession, 1537. Edward's half-sister, Princess Mary follows him, with a lady-in-waiting carrying her train

Right: Edward VI, English School, c1575

King Edward. y.e VI.

PARVLE PATRISSA, PATRIS VIRTVTIS ET HAERES
ESTO, NIHIL MAIVS MAXIMVS ORBIS HABET.
GNATVM VIX POSSVNT COELVM ET NATVRA DEDISSE
HVIVS QVEM PATRIS, VICTVS HONORET HONOS.
AEQVATO TANTVM, TANTI TV FACTA PARENTIS,
VOTA HOMINVM, VIX QVO PROGREDIANTVR, HABENT
VINCITO, QVOT REGES PRIS

Portrait of Edward as a baby, by Hans Holbein the Younger, c1538

Whipping boy Among Edward's fellow scholars was his favourite friend Barnaby Fitzpatrick, who became his whipping boy. If Edward was naughty, Barnaby was punished. If Barnaby was naughty, Barnaby was punished.

King Edward On 28 January 1547 Henry VIII died. The next day Edward and Elizabeth, who had been hustled away to Enfield, were told the news. They clung to each other, sobbing; what would become of them, children as they were? The new king was under the protection of his maternal uncle Edward Seymour, earl of Hertford, who was to become the Protector during Edward's minority. On 20 February Edward was crowned, after processing from the Tower to Westminster; this was the first Protestant coronation, and anti-papal messages peppered the ceremony, although it was shortened since the King was but a boy.

Edward VI and the Pope, c1575, English School. This is an allegory of the Reformation, with Henry VIII directing from death, while his heir and other key figures continue his good work. The enlarged scene shows the destruction of holy images

| Henry VIII | The Pope | The Bible | Edward VI | Edward Seymour, Duke of Somerset | Thomas Cranm |

The Coronation Procession of King Edward VI in 1547 by Grimm, 1785

Somerset rises, and falls Then it was time to go back to lessons. Seymour meanwhile had been made Duke of Somerset, and he ruled England disastrously. By 1549 the country was nearly bankrupt, and a palace coup in October removed him from power.

Almost uniquely in royal history, the young Edward kept a journal, a mixture of high-minded thoughts and childish fancies. The phrase 'booted and spurred' is first recorded in it. Edward recorded drily in the journal what happened in 1549. He was kept at Hampton Court in Somerset's custody, and 500 guards were armed and armoured against attack. Edward was then spirited away to Windsor Castle, but with little provision there the beleaguered court was almost starved out. 'Methinks I was in prison', Edward wrote. On 11 October Somerset capitulated and was arrested, charged, as Edward recorded in his journal with 'ambition, vainglory, entering into rash wars in mine youth, negligent looking on Newhaven, enriching himself of my treasure, following his own opinion, and doing all by his own authority, etc.' He was eventually executed in January 1552.

Northumberland rules By then, a collective governorship was in place led by John Dudley, Earl of Warwick, who became Duke of Northumberland in 1551. His rule was much more successful: wars were ended, financially prudent policies were followed, overseas debts were liquidated, peace

was restored. By this time, Edward was growing in assertiveness, making his thoughts and opinions known. He hastened the pace of religious reform, inspired by the Protestant zeal he had been given by his tutors from an early age.

Unhappy end The boy who had once been so strong sickened quickly in the early months of 1553. He caught a cold, then measles, and finally it was clear he was dying from tuberculosis. On 6 July he died, at Greenwich, and he was buried in Westminster Abbey on 8 August.

Succession Once again, the succession was an issue. Edward had taken against his elder half-sister Mary for her Catholicism; and he considered neither she nor Elizabeth should or could succeed him as they were women. In the end he had devised a formula that gave the throne to the male heirs of his Protestant cousin once removed Jane Grey, but this was thwarted by his death. Jane would succeed him for only nine days before Henry VIII's direct blood line reasserted itself in his half-sister Mary.

Legacy With his encouragement, the foundation had been laid for a great transformation in society, the Protestant reformation. In the six years that followed his half-sister Mary failed to win back the hearts and minds of the people. If Edward had lived, the course of history may have been very different indeed.

43

Politics and protection

Edward VI's reign was one of difficulty from beginning to end. Not only was a boy on the throne, but the country was racked by disease, poverty and harvest failure. Beggars roamed the lanes and streets, and were treated mercilessly.

Crisis after crisis Wars drained the coffers. Protector Somerset tried diplomacy first – when he was only 6 Edward was betrothed to the 7-months-old Mary Queen of Scots – but that failed and war followed. By 1549 England was at war with both Scotland and France, and the huge cost led to desperate measures being taken. The coinage was debased, religious chantries were sold off as the monasteries had once been, and a tax on sheep was levied, but this was still nowhere enough.

1549 was the year everything went wrong, and the regime was tested to the limit. Armed risings took place in different parts of the country, fed by religious feeling mixed with acute economic distress. In Devon and Cornwall, people rose against the new Prayer Book in English. Kett's Rebellion in Norfolk mixed religious anxieties with protest against economic and social injustice, notably the encroachment by landlords onto common grazing land. Dudley crushed the Norfolk rebellion, and used that as a springboard to bring down Somerset.

After the coup Somerset fell from power, Northumberland took the reins, and conditions improved. Even so, further attempted coups happened, the royal court was militarised, and everyone was fearful for the future. Better and less divisive government was instituted, including establishing lords lieutenant in each county as permanent representatives of the Crown. Peace with France and Scotland, a temporary end to some of the worst food crises, financial prudence, better coinage and debt being paid off all made a contribution to greater stability after the mid-century crisis.

A 16th-century woodcut of the execution of the Duke of Somerset on Tower Hill, 22 January, 1552

John Dudley, Duke of Northumberland, engraved by H T Ryall, 1836, after Hans Holbein

Religion and succession

Henry VIII's reformation had not been a very Protestant one; the old Catholic ways survived for the most part. The real change came under Edward. Archbishop Thomas Cranmer introduced the Book of Common Prayer in 1549, following a strong wave of iconoclasm and enforced change over the previous two years. Images were removed, stained glass windows were smashed, chantries where masses were said for the souls of the dead – and, crucially, their schools – were abolished, their rights and properties sold to the highest bidders. Edward himself helped lead the change to Protestantism.

Reaction was at times bewildered, and often violent. When the use of the Book of Common Prayer was enforced, the west of England rose in open revolt. Landowners led their tenantry into pitched battles, especially around Exeter. The loss of life was on a scale not to be repeated until the Civil War of the 1640s. Undeterred, Edward's government pressed on, introducing a new and more radical Prayer Book in 1552, and a new Act of Uniformity designed to enforce the new orthodoxy.

In Mary's reign, attempts were made to unpick what Edward and his advisers had achieved; but they failed, and England remained a Protestant nation.

Edward's chosen successor By March 1553 Edward had written a 'Devise for the Succession', a sort of will that looked to who would follow him: all good Protestants, and his distant cousin Lady Jane Grey was preferred. The driving force in this seems to have been his own. His successor should be a Protestant, and the claims of his half-sisters Mary and Elizabeth were passed over as they were either Catholic or a woman or both. In choosing Jane Grey, his cousin once removed on his mother's side, he specified that her male heirs would succeed. As his death approached, Edward was persuaded to swallow his scruples and allow a woman to succeed him.

Narrative print showing the coronation of Edward VI, the Pope being banished and 'true religion' restored, and the Duke of Somerset's execution. English School, 16th century

Edward was persuaded to swallow his scruples to allow Lady Jane Grey to succeed him

Lady Jane Grey, by an unknown artist, late 16th century

Lady Jane Grey
1553

Queue for nine days

Useful factfile

Born 1537 at Bradgate Manor, Leicestershire

Married Guildford Dudley, 1553

Proclaimed Queen 10 July 1553

Died Executed for treason 12 February 1554, aged 17. Buried Tower of London

Parents Duke of Suffolk and Lady Frances Brandon

Short and sad Lady Jane Grey, or Lady Jane Dudley, or Queen Jane: her reign from 10-19 July 1553 was the shortest in English history. She was to be a puppet of her father-in-law, John Dudley, Duke of Northumberland, who had effectively ruled England in the last years of Edward VI's reign. Jane's claim was a blood one, as she was a great-grand-daughter of Henry VII by his younger daughter Mary, who had been Queen of France briefly and then Duchess of Suffolk. As the wife of Guildford Dudley, Northumberland's son, she was now in his family. And as a devout and intelligent Protestant, she fitted the succession issue well. Edward named her in his 'Devise for the Succession'.

A reluctant queen The Privy Council withdrew their support for Jane only nine days after she was proclaimed, alarmed at the extent of popular and armed support for Mary and fearful of the consequences of deviating so far from a true line of succession. Jane was an unwilling monarch, and although condemned for high treason her life was initially spared and she was imprisoned in the Tower of London, along with her husband Guildford.

A narrative print of the life of Lady Jane Grey, English School, 17th century

The Execution of Lady Jane Grey by Paul Delaroche, 1833

Mary's mercy The former queen and her husband were tried and condemned as traitors at the Guildhall in November 1553. Queen Mary was merciful and granted a reprieve from the death penalty, allowing the couple to remain high-status prisoners of the Tower.

Test of faith However, Thomas Wyatt's armed Protestant rebellion of January 1554 made Jane's existence far more of a threat to the Queen. The involvement of her father in the rebellion sealed Jane's fate. Mary could not afford to let her live, although the Queen offered to spare their lives on condition that they converted to the Catholic faith. Both refused and were condemned to death.

Jane's final hours On 12 February 1554 her husband Guildford Dudley was publicly executed on Tower Hill at 10 am. According to the anonymous *Chronicle of Queen Jane and two years of Queen Mary*, Jane saw him from her window being led to his execution and the decapitated corpse return afterwards. She was led to her own execution an hour later. As one of the privileged few, Jane was beheaded within the Tower walls, on a scaffold erected next to the White Tower. She was 17 years old. The pitiful scene of her execution became a favourite subject of 19th-century romantic artists, such as the famous scene imagined by Paul Delaroche, above.

Mary I
1553-8

Obsessively pious, a psychological mess, with a 'tin ear' for public opinion

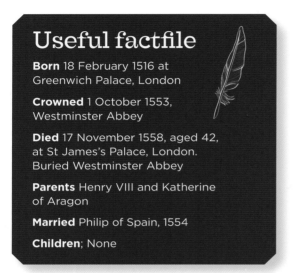

Useful factfile

Born 18 February 1516 at Greenwich Palace, London

Crowned 1 October 1553, Westminster Abbey

Died 17 November 1558, aged 42, at St James's Palace, London. Buried Westminster Abbey

Parents Henry VIII and Katherine of Aragon

Married Philip of Spain, 1554

Children; None

The fight for power The first obstacle to the succession of Mary, Edward's elder half-sister, was that she was a woman. There had never been a reigning queen (with the possible exception of Matilda in the 12th century), and all Henry VIII's marital endeavours had been to secure a male heir. The second obstacle was that the dying Edward had named someone else as his successor, Jane Grey, daughter-in-law of his protector the Duke of Northumberland. She too was a woman; but crucially she was Protestant, and Mary was a zealous Catholic.

Jane had not wanted to be queen, but forces rallied to Mary at her power base in Norfolk with her claim of birth and right, and after nine days Henry's daughter won the day. A woman was now fully on the throne. On her victory march into London Mary was accompanied by her half-sister Elizabeth. And soon poor Jane and her husband Guildford Dudley were to be executed at the Tower for treason (see page 48).

Not a looker Mary was small and short-sighted, 'mannish' in some descriptions with a very deep voice. She may have also had a form of rhinitis that gave her foul smelling breath, and other health problems that may have given her problems conceiving. A visiting ambassador described her as being 'of low stature, with red and white complexion, and very thin. Her eyes are white and large and her hair reddish'.

Finest moment Her speech to Parliament in the desperate hours of 1554, as rebels headed by Sir Thomas Wyatt marched on the capital. Citizens of London remained unconvinced, but her troops stayed loyal and the rebels were routed.

Miniature of Princess Mary, attributed to Lucas Horenbout, c1525

ANNO DNI

LADI MARI
THE MOST
KING HENRI

THE AGE OF

Princess Mary (later Mary I),
by Master John, 1544

Palace connections

Mary was at **Hampton Court Palace** in 1554 when the Spanish ambassadors arrive to offer her the hand of King Phillip of Spain, which she accepted despite all the bad omens and popular opposition. A year later the court, an uneasy mix of Spanish and English courtiers, gathered at the palace to await the birth of Mary's baby. Her younger half sister, Princess Elizabeth, was summoned and kept under close guard.
However, the baby never came; Mary's swollen belly was possibly the result of a psychological 'phantom pregnancy'.

Silver medal showing
Mary I, by Jacopo da
Trezzo, c1555

Philip II of Spain and Mary I by Hans Eworth, 1558

Unhappy end On 7 January 1558, England lost Calais, its final area of land on French soil, to the forces of the Duke of Guise. By the end of the year Mary was dead, probably a victim of the cancer that had previously led her to believe she had been pregnant. She had become reconciled to her sister Elizabeth, who succeeded her on 17 November.

What kind of ruler?

In some areas of public life, Mary's reign had positive effects. The government had taken further steps towards reversing inflation, including a re-coinage that would have a lasting impact, reducing levels of government expenditure, and instituting reforms in town government. The commercial potential of market expansion into Eastern Europe and Africa began to be realised. But in five short, bloody years, the proud and bitter Queen had alienated her nation.

Worst mistake Almost every step she made proved to be faulty. Her initial popularity among the people soon dissolved when she announced that she intended to marry her cousin Prince Philip of Spain (see page 54), who was soon to succeed to the Habsburg lands and royal titles. This stirred up huge anti-Spanish, and anti-Catholic sentiment.

Mary's marriage. Mary would not be dissuaded against a Spanish alliance and Winchester Cathedral was the setting for the wedding on 25 July 1554. This was far from a match made in heaven, for Philip did not care for his bride, spent little time with her, grew impatient at her series of phantom pregnancies, and inherited the Spanish throne himself in 1556.

A Protestant plot The marriage alliance with Spain was deeply unpopular, and in 1554 the first of a series of Protestant rebellions was led by Thomas Wyatt. The rebels' intention was to place Mary's Protestant half-sister, Princess Elizabeth on the throne instead; when their plan was discovered, they were hunted down, and Wyatt was tortured to persuade him to say that Elizabeth herself had been involved. Mary could then have had her rival executed for treason. But Wyatt never implicated Elizabeth, and he went to the scaffold without her, although Elizabeth was kept a prisoner, including a period in the Tower (see page 59).

Sir Thomas Wyatt, after Hans Holbein the Younger, c1540

In five short,
bloody years
the proud,
bitter Queen
had alienated
the nation

Queen Mary I,
by Antonio Moro,
1554

53

Philip II of Spain, by an
unknown artist, c1580

Philip of Spain

A reluctant husband who returned to his native land to rule as soon as he could.

Useful factfile

Born 21 May 1527 at Valladolid, Spain

Crowned (King of England) 1554

Married (1) Maria of Portugal 1543-45, (2) Mary I of England, 1554-8 (no children), (3) Elizabeth de Valois 1550-68, (4) Anna of Austria, 1570-80

Died 13 September 1598. Buried El Escorial

Parents Charles V, Holy Roman Emperor and Isabella of Portugal

What kind of ruler? In Spain, the reign of King Philip II is known as the Golden Age, when the Spanish empire reached the peak of its power and wealth, and the Habsburg monarch ruled lands from the Netherlands, Spain, Portugal, Naples, Sicily and Milan to South and Central America and the Pacific.

He acquired all his titles between 1554 and 1581. For the first four of those years he was also king of England, as consort to Mary I, although he was never allowed to exercise power, much to his displeasure.

Personal style Shy and reserved, good at history but very poor at languages, so despite his extensive travels he found it hard to make a powerful impression.

Interested in? Philip was deeply passionate about collecting rare books and art.

Religious monument Philip and Mary were both keenly and deeply religious. His own greatest monument is the monastery-palace of El Escorial outside Madrid, where the ascetic monarch ruled a world empire from a small study bedroom with a private view to the high altar below.

Impact on England? Muted and constrained. Philip was given no jurisdiction, which he deeply resented. He came to despise his wife, who failed time and again to produce a child, and he disdained the English with their often uncouth ways. Yet Mary loved him, and was distraught after his departure in 1555 to defend his realms in Flanders. He rarely returned to England and his wife thereafter, especially once he had succeeded to the Spanish throne in 1556, except to lobby for war as he did in 1557.

Legacy What he did give Mary was their joint title, probably the grandest in all English history: Philip and Mary, by the Grace of God King and Queen of England, Spain, France, Jerusalem, both the Sicilies and Ireland, Defenders of the Faith, Archdukes of Austria, Dukes of Burgundy, Milan and Brabant, Counts of Habsburg, Flanders and Tirol.

> Philip came to despise his wife, who failed to produce a child, and he disdained the English with their uncouth ways

'Bloody Mary': politics and religion

Catholicism revived Both Mary and Philip were devout and devoted Catholics, and their religious ideals had enormous consequences for their respective nations. Mary was determined to return her realm to the true faith. Images, vestments and liturgy were restored in churches, Protestant clergy were forced to repudiate their wives, and the tenets of the new religion established under Edward VI were reversed. Many stouter Protestants fled overseas, where they were influenced by the stricter doctrines being developed in Geneva and elsewhere. There was neither opportunity nor money to return the monasteries and chantries to monks and nuns, but there was a campaign of religious terror to wage instead.

Above: The martyrdom of Sir Thomas Cranmer from Foxe's *Book of Martyrs*

Below: An English Protestant being racked during Mary I's reign; from Foxe's *Book of Martyrs*

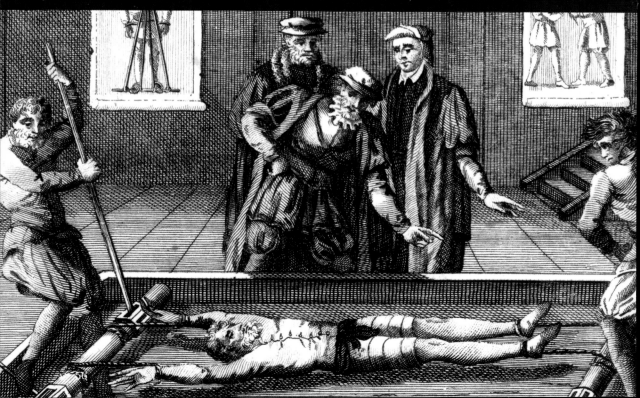

Bloody Mary Mary's weapons in the fight were not secret. They were torture and execution. Foxe's *Book of Martyrs,* first published in 1563 and reprinted many times, famously and gruesomely described and depicted the victims of the Marian efforts to defeat Protestantism, with prisoners stretched on the rack or burnt at the stake (see page 92). Over 280 dissenters were executed for heresy in Mary's brief reign, including Archbishop Cranmer who was one of the so-called Oxford Martyrs along with Bishops Ridley and Latimer.

The numbers of burnings increased annually, and led to a tide of popular revulsion. Creating martyrs such as Cranmer only helped shore up the reformers' cause, exemplified by the words said to have been uttered by Bishop Hugh Latimer to his fellow bishop Nicholas Ridley as the fires were lit beneath them: 'Be of good comfort, Master Ridley, and play the man. We shall this day light such a candle, by God's grace in England as I trust shall never be put out.' But Mary was undaunted and the burning policy was continued throughout her reign. However, the Reformation in England had picked up too much momentum to be stopped in its tracks.

Cardinal Pole Cardinal Reginald Pole was the last Catholic Archbishop of Canterbury and the last Cardinal to have extraordinary political power in England. On his return from exile he became one of Mary's closest advisers.

Pole was a man with royal blood. His grandfather was the ill-fated Duke of Clarence (who was, allegedly, drowned in a barrel of Malmsey), brother of Richard III; his mother Margaret was Countess of Salisbury and the last of the Plantagenets, who in her extreme old age had been sent to the execution scaffold by Henry VIII. The family, including Reginald, had broken with Henry VIII over his first divorce. In 1537, although he was not yet ordained, Pole was made a cardinal by Pope Paul III. He remained in exile, plotting for Catholic victories, until the death of Edward VI when he was made papal legate – ambassador – and came back to England.

Pole became Mary I's principal political and religious adviser, and he shares with her the blame for the tide of executions for heresy that were intended to help bring England back to the Catholic fold and ultimately had the opposite effect.

Unhappy end Pole died within hours of his royal mistress in 1558, a victim of the great influenza epidemic that had an even more devastating effect on the population than did the burnings.

Reginald Pole, by an unknown artist, *c*1556

Bishops Nicholas Ridley and Hugh Latimer burnt at the stake near the gates of Balliol, Oxford in 1555, from Foxe's *Book of Martyrs*

Queen Elizabeth I, by an unknown artist, *c*1600. Known as 'The Coronation Portrait', it shows the Queen in cloth of gold and holding the orb and sceptre, symbols of her authority

Elizabeth I
1558-1603

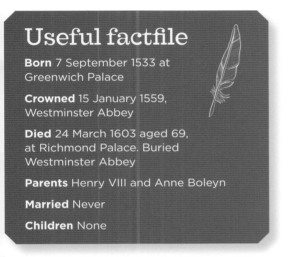

Intelligent, yet indecisive – a consummate politician and ultimate survivor

Early life tragedy From being the apple of her father's eye, the little Princess's life was thrown into disarray when at age three, her mother Anne Boleyn was executed, Elizabeth was declared a bastard and removed from her father's presence.

Back in favour Elizabeth was largely brought up at Hatfield House in Hertfordshire, although she did attend court on occasions. With the birth of an heir with his new wife Jane Seymour, Henry could afford once again to be magnanimous to his clever, red-haired daughter. Henry's sixth wife, Kateryn Parr treated Elizabeth as her own daughter, furthering her education with a series of excellent tutors.

Playing for time As a young woman, Protestant Elizabeth was a potential threat to Catholic Queen Mary I. Her life was marred with instability, as she fell in and out of her sister's favour and she lived in the shadow of imprisonment, or worse. She learnt the valuable skill of procrastination, although this fear of committing herself may have made her indecisive as sovereign.

Love of learning Elizabeth's tutors included the brilliant humanist scholar Roger Ascham, who found her a serious and rewarding student. The Princess mastered not only Latin and Greek, but also Italian, French and Spanish.

Princess in peril Elizabeth survived some sticky moments before becoming queen. After her father's death, she went to live with her stepmother Kateryn and Kateryn's new husband Thomas Seymour, who it is believed sexually abused the young princess. When Kateryn died in childbirth, the lecherous and supremely ambitious Seymour tried to marry the Princess himself as a possible route to power. Elizabeth wisely prevaricated, and in 1549 Seymour was charged with treason against Edward VI. Elizabeth was subjected to humiliating and intensive interrogation, but gave nothing away to implicate herself.

A narrow escape In 1554, despite her show of support for her half-sister Mary, Elizabeth was arrested and charged with complicity in Sir Thomas Wyatt's rebellion. As the focus of Protestant discontent, Elizabeth was incarcerated and questioned in the Tower, while the captured rebel leaders were horribly tortured to extract evidence against her. They gave nothing away. Again, Elizabeth kept her nerve. The Queen's advisers recommended Elizabeth be executed, but Mary spared her half-sister to a year's house arrest.

A welcome succession After Mary I and Philip of Spain failed to produce an heir, the throne was Elizabeth's. The news of Elizabeth's succession was greeted with great rejoicing as people looked forward to freedom from religious persecution. Bells rang out from every church and bonfires blazed across England.

Personal style The young queen was described as 'a lady upon whom nature had bestowed, and well placed, many of her fairest favours'. She had extravagant tastes, owning over 3000 magnificent dresses, many embroidered with gold thread and encrusted with jewels. As she aged, she fought a valiant battle, wearing elaborate wigs to cover her thinning hair, painting white lead onto her face to hide smallpox scars and rubbing urine into wrinkles. However, she was unable to resist sugar, which caused her teeth to rot and blacken.

Energetic Elizabeth On occasion the Queen liked to throw off the decorum of monarchy in private. She ordered that the palace windows overlooking her Privy Garden and Pond Garden at Hampton Court be blocked up so that 'her majesty shall walk secretly all hours and times without any looking upon her out of any place'. On cold mornings she would march about the heraldic garden with great vigour 'to catch her heate'.

Tolerant… up to a point On her succession Elizabeth declared herself against religious persecution, saying she didn't want to 'make windows into men's souls'. However, her subjects were heavily fined if they didn't attend Church of England services, and after 1570 when the Pope declared Elizabeth to be deposed, being an active Catholic became an offence punishable by death.

Greatest achievement To keep England from civil war and maintain the country's integrity as a sovereign state in Europe after the break with Rome. Her regime finally buckled under the pressures of war, and by the end of her reign the country was bedevilled by poor economic conditions and bad harvests, distress fuelled by soaring population growth, despite the myth of 'Elizabeth the magnificent'.

Palace connections

As a princess, Elizabeth was imprisoned at the Tower of London for a frightening few months in 1554, suspected of involvement in a Protestant rebellion against her Catholic half-sister Mary I. Five years later Elizabeth returned in triumph to the Tower to spend the night before her coronation. Elizabeth was fond of **Hampton Court Palace** and while she didn't add substantially to the palace, she commissioned several 'marvels', including a legendary glittering 'Paradise Room' decorated with precious metals and gems to dazzle visitors. She was also fond of practical jokes, and installed a fountain that squirted water at unsuspecting passers-by!

What kind of ruler?

Elizabeth was often indecisive (perhaps as a result of the doubts and dangers of her early years) and her ambiguity often infuriated her advisers. But she could also be very astute and clear when political considerations demanded it. She perceived that her role must be that of a Protestant sovereign, whatever her private beliefs. Despite several failed attempts to make a political marriage, Elizabeth eventually chose the single life, enjoying the attention of several favourites and using trusted advisers to guide her Protestant kingdom through troubled times.

Elizabeth I when a Princess, at the age of about 13, *c*1546 attributed to William Scrots

Elizabeth's men
The Advisers

The Queen liked to be surrounded by those who complimented her; she was a flirt and enjoyed her favourites dancing attendance upon her. However, she was intelligent and astute, choosing superb and loyal advisers. She remained famously undecided over making a political marriage, although she probably took several lovers. She eventually became, symbolically, 'the Virgin Queen' – married to her country.

Elizabeth I in the allegorical 'Rainbow Portrait' symbolising peace and prosperity, by Isaac Oliver, c1600

Key to understanding Elizabeth is the role of her special advisers. Wise and experienced, although rivalrous with each other, they were loyal to the queen. By contrast, her courtiers came and went. Elizabeth kept the politics of the court separate from the serious business of ruling in the real world.

William Cecil
1520-98

Cecil had served on Edward VI's Privy Council. Elizabeth made him her private secretary and principal secretary of state on her accession in 1558. He was created Baron Burghley in 1571 and was a tireless and loyal minister until his death, advising the Queen cautiously yet decisively. She nicknamed him her 'Spirit'. As an elderly man he suffered from gout but was still valuable to Elizabeth, who told him 'My lord, we make use of you, not for your bad legs, but for your good head'.

'My lord, we make use of you, not for your bad legs, but for your good head'

William Cecil by an unknown Anglo-Netherlandish artist, 1560s

Robert Cecil
1563-1612

William's son Robert attended Elizabeth in her later years and succeeded his father as principal adviser. Elizabeth continued to assert herself as queen, despite her failing energy and strength, but the younger man had not inherited his father's diplomacy. When he advised that she must go to bed when she was feeling ill, she famously crushed him: 'Must? Is must a word to be used to princes? Little man, little man, thy father, if he had been alive, durst not have used that word.'

> **'Must? Is must a word to be used to princes? Little man, little man, thy father, if he had been alive, durst not have used that word'**

Robert Cecil, 1st Earl of Salisbury, by John De Critz the Elder, 1602

Francis Walsingham
*c*1530-90

Elizabeth's 'spymaster'. Appointed principal secretary in 1573, Protestant Walsingham had fled Mary I's persecution and lived in exile in Europe, travelling and building anti-Catholic contacts. Under Elizabeth he wielded great power and influence, and oversaw a skilled network of informers and code breakers working to foil Catholic plots, including Arthur Gregory who could break and invisibly re-make seals on letters! While ambassador to Paris, Walsingham witnessed the 1572 St Bartholomew's Day massacre of Protestant Huguenots by Catholics, and dedicated himself to preventing any similar atrocity in England. Elizabeth valued and listened to his advice, even when unwelcome, such as when he counselled against marrying foreign princes, and most notably when he advised the queen to execute her cousin, Mary Queen of Scots (see page 66) to prevent further plots.

Sir Francis Walsingham, thought to be by John De Critz the Elder, *c*1587

Elizabeth's men
The 'Lovers'

Elizabeth allowed herself to be 'wooed and courted, and even had love made to her' by a succession of favourites. However, she always kept the upper hand.

Robert Dudley
1532-88

Earl of Leicester, whom Elizabeth nicknamed 'Sweet Robin'. In the first 18 months of her reign he was always at court and also, gossip had it, frequently in the Queen's bedchamber. There was talk of marriage. However, Robert was already married to Amy Robsart, who then died in what was ruled an 'accidental', rather than suicidal, fall down a flight of stairs. Scandal swirled, and after hesitating, Elizabeth decided marriage to Dudley was too dangerous.

Sir Christopher Hatton
1540-91

This tall, handsome lawyer first caught Elizabeth's eye in 1561 when she saw him playing 'Master of the Game' in a masque. He was an excellent dancer, too. Elizabeth appointed him vice-chancellor of the royal household, knighted him, and showered him with valuable grants and other appointments. There were claims that he was her lover; they were undoubtedly close friends, and Elizabeth visited him on his deathbed.

Robert Dudley, Earl of Leicester, attributed to Steven van der Meulen, c1560-65

Sir Walter Ralegh
*c*1552-1618

Adventurer, courtier, navigator, author and poet,
who came to the Queen's attention in 1580 when
he helped suppress an Irish uprising. Elizabeth
knighted Ralegh, made him a Captain of the
Queen's Guard, and he was soon a firm favourite.
However, in 1592 the Queen discovered he had
secretly married Elizabeth Throckmorton, one
of her maids of honour. Furious, she had the couple
imprisoned in the Tower. They were were eventually
released and Ralegh returned to favour, but after
the Queen's death he fell foul of James I, and was
once again sent to the Tower. He was executed for
treason in 1618.

Robert Devereux,
Earl of Essex
1565-1601

Elizabeth's last favourite, the cocky Devereux
was shown great favour until he returned without
permission from an unsuccessful campaign to put
down a rebellion in Ireland in 1599. He was found guilty
of dereliction of duty and put under house arrest,
whereupon he attempted a ridiculously unsuccessful
coup and was executed for treason in 1601.

Other 'official' suitors Elizabeth used other courtships
as a pretext to conduct diplomatic negotiations with
foreign powers, and she probably enjoyed playing off
her 'suitors' against each other. She seemed to like the
Duke of Anjou most of all, wined and dined him and
his entourage and put on a seemingly amorous show.

But the canny Queen, after seeing at first hand the
problems her half-sister Mary I encountered after
marrying Philip of Spain, was fearful of subjection,
and particularly of a Catholic husband. She finally
rejected all candidates, including members of the
English nobility, as this would have shown favour
to one aristocratic family over another. Her own
temperament, as well as her desire to protect her
country, probably influenced her decision. She once
told Robert Dudley, when he had pushed her too
far, 'God's death, my lord, I will have here but one
mistress and no master.'

*A Young Man Leaning
Against A Tree Amongst
Roses*, 1585-95, thought
to be Robert Devereux,
by Nicholas Hilliard

Catholic plots

In the first decade of Elizabeth's reign Catholic Spain sought to maintain good trade relations with Protestant England; and at home Elizabeth pursued her 'middle way', showing religious tolerance. However, Elizabeth knew in fact that Catholics abroad, and nearer home, were all potential enemies.

The Northern Rising In 1568, the powerful Catholic earls of Northumberland and Westmorland led an uprising, marching on York after celebrating the illegal Catholic Mass at Durham Cathedral. Although it was quickly suppressed by forces loyal to Elizabeth, the rebellion encouraged other Catholics, most notably the Pope, to seize the moment.

Elizabeth is excommunicated In 1570 Pope Pius V, probably encouraged by the Northern Rising, issued a bull excommunicating Elizabeth, declaring her 'to be deprived of her pretended title' – in effect granting permission to her own Catholic subjects and to the Catholic powers of Europe to seek the overthrow of the English queen. And Elizabeth's own cousin, Mary, Queen of Scots, provided the focus of such plots.

Catholics abroad, and nearer home, were all potential enemies to Elizabeth

Mary, Queen of Scots

Early life Mary, daughter of James V of Scotland and his French queen, Mary of Guise, became queen on the death of her father when she was only 6 days old. Her mother acted as regent. In the interests of French/Scottish diplomacy, young Mary was betrothed to the Dauphin, and was brought up as a Catholic in the French court.

Return to Scotland Mary married the Dauphin in 1558 but was widowed two years later at 18 and so returned to Scotland. Although a Catholic, Mary accepted the Protestant-led government and initially ruled with moderation. However, she made enemies through a series of bad decisions and un-regal behaviour. Her second husband Lord Darnley was murdered in 1565; Mary was forced to abdicate in 1567 and their infant son James was made king.

Flight to England Mary was imprisoned in Lochleven Castle, Kinross-shire. She escaped in 1568, only for her army to be defeated at the Battle of Langside near Glasgow, Mary fled to England to seek refuge with her cousin, Elizabeth I.

The trouble with Mary Aware that her cousin presented a dangerous threat, Elizabeth had her put under house arrest and kept under surveillance. Over the next 19 years, inevitably Mary became the focus of numerous Catholic plots to depose Elizabeth and make her queen. But as her cousin appeared not to be directly involved in these plots Elizabeth refused to act against her.

Proof Then in 1586, Francis Walsingham intercepted letters between Mary and Anthony Babington who was plotting to depose Elizabeth. This evidence convinced Elizabeth that, while she lived, Mary would always be dangerous. Mary was tried for treason and condemned to death in October 1586, although Elizabeth agonised over signing her death warrant for several months.

Unhappy end Mary was executed at Fotheringhay Castle, Northamptonshire, on 8 February 1587 at the age of 44. It is said that Elizabeth was deeply distressed.

PRINCEPS ET HERES LEGITIMA IACOBI MAGNA BRITAN
NIA REGIS MATER, QVAM SVORVM HARESI VEXATAM
REBELLIONE OPPRESSAM, RETVGI CAVSA VERBO ELIZ
REGINA ET COGNATA INNIXAM IN ANGLIAM AN
1568 DESCENDENTEM 19 AN CAPTIVAM PER
FIDIA DETINVIT MILLEQ CALVMNYS TRADVXIT
GRVDELI SENATVS ANGLICI SENTENTIA
HARESI INSTIGANTE NECI TRADITVR
AC 12 KAL MARTI 1587 A SERVILI
CARNIFICE OBTRVNCATVR AN°
ATAT REGNIQ 45

MY
FODRINGHA

IAM SERENISS REGVM
M VXOREM ET MATREM
NTIBVS COMMISSARIIS
NISTRIS R ELI CAR
X SECVRI PERCVIIT :
VNO ET ALTERO
TRVCVLENTER SAV
TERTIO EI CAPVT
ABSCINDIT

Mary, Queen of Scots, British School, *c*1610-40. In this pro-Catholic portrait,
Mary is in mourning costume below the Royal Arms of Scotland. Behind her
are two of her ladies; to the left a graphic scene of her execution

Elizabeth and the Armada

The death of Mary, Queen of Scots did not remove the threat to Protestant England from Catholic adversaries. In 1586 Elizabeth was confronted with her biggest challenge yet – a Spanish invasion.

What sparked it off? In contrast to her father Henry VIII, Elizabeth was reluctant to get involved in foreign wars. She maintained peace by diplomacy, playing off the two major powers of France and Spain against each other. However, the terrible persecution of Protestants on the Continent meant that in 1582 she had agreed to give military support to the Dutch revolt against Spain. This, combined with the execution of Mary, Queen of Scots plus attacks by English 'pirates' on Spanish ships returning from the New World, provoked Philip II of Spain into retaliating.

The Spanish are coming! Elizabeth's vigilant spymaster Francis Walsingham used his talents to develop an extensive network of 'intelligencers' all over Europe and the Mediterranean. In 1586 his agents informed him that the Spanish were preparing to invade. Preparations were made to fortify England, including work at Dover harbour, and a fleet was prepared.

The attack Despite English tactics to distract and delay the Spanish, a huge fleet of 130 ships set sail from Lisbon in July 1588, under the command of the Duke of Medina Sidonia. The fleet planned to sail up the English Channel, pick up Spanish troops waiting on shore at Flanders, then cross to England. However, English ships were faster and more agile in the water, and they isolated and picked off Spanish vessels as

they sailed. Eventually the Spanish anchored off Calais, but they were attacked throughout the night by English fireships. Driven out to sea, the weakened Spaniards suffered huge losses when they finally engaged with the English vessels.

Elizabeth's finest hour Meanwhile, the English prepared for invasion. When the Spanish fleet were sighted off Cornwall, beacon fires were lit across the kingdom. The Queen rode out to address her troops at Tilbury, seizing the moment to make her magnificent, frequently quoted speech:

English ships and the Spanish Armada August 1588, British School, 16th century

'I know I have the body of a weak and feeble woman, but I have the heart and stomach of a king, and a king of England too ...'

Victory! The weather became England's greatest ally – southerly winds gained strength and the large, heavy Spanish ships found it almost impossible to get back to Calais, and were forced to sail north in a worsening storm. More ships were lost on the rocky coasts of Ireland and Scotland; thousands of men perished. Despite the weather playing the decisive role, the destruction of the Spanish Armada boosted English national pride for years, and cemented the legend of 'Gloriana'.

Queen Elizabeth I being carried in Procession (Eliza Triumphans), attributed to Robert Peake, c1601

An Elizabethan Golden Age

Elizabethan London's first purpose-built theatre was the Globe, created in 1576, as shown in this 17th-century English engraving

At the time, and ever since, the reign of Elizabeth I – for all its dangers and the crises that rocked it – has been regarded as an age of gold. It saw the flowering of poetry, music and literature, a new architecture was born, and painting and portraiture entered new realms of endeavour.

Above all, the Elizabethan era is most famous for theatre, as William Shakespeare, Christopher Marlowe and others broke free of past styles and created some of the greatest stage works ever known. This was also an age of exploration and expansion abroad, while at home, the Protestant Reformation became acceptable to most, particularly after the Spanish Armada of 1588 was repulsed.

Gloriana So much of the art and literature of the age revolved round the cult of Gloriana, Elizabeth the Virgin Queen who ruled an ever-greater nation and commanded the adoration of her courtiers. In Catholic England the Virgin Mary had that status, now it was transferred into a secular sphere. Idealised in portraits as a goddess, and idolised in poetry and song as a virginal embodiment of the virtues, her image was carefully crafted.

Even as an old woman she was portrayed as eternally youthful. If the portraits of her all look basically the same, that is because there was an official model face for artists to copy, around which they arranged the sumptuous jewels and clothes she wore and the allegorical themes she embodied. By refusing to marry, Elizabeth side-stepped the issue of succession, and she turned that to political advantage. She explained, 'I keep the good will of all my husbands — my good people'.

Music and theatre Some of the greatest English composers before the modern age flourished in the reign of Elizabeth: William Byrd, Thomas Tallis and Thomas Campion among them. Religious music, songs and ayres, instrumental solo and ensemble works flowed from their pens.

As London expanded, so the theatres grew in number and status from the 1570s, and many great works – tragical, comical, historical, pastoral – including Shakespeare's *Midsummer Night's Dream* and *Hamlet* and Christopher Marlowe's *Dr Faustus*, were written in the 1590s.

> The Elizabethan era is most famous for theatre, as William Shakespeare and Christopher Marlowe created some of the greatest stage works ever known

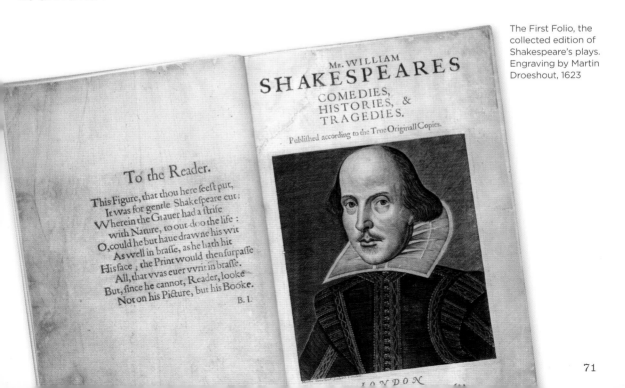

The First Folio, the collected edition of Shakespeare's plays. Engraving by Martin Droeshout, 1623

Longleat House in Wiltshire,
built c1580 by Sir John Thynne.
This 17th century image, *A View
of Longleat,* is by Jans Silberechts

Architecture and technology The Italian Renaissance was running its course by the reign of Elizabeth, but a new Renaissance was being experienced in England. Less classically pure than its European manifestation, bringing together many different influences, new buildings expressed a peaceful and expansionist age. Many of the greatest buildings are associated with Robert Smythson, especially the 'prodigy houses' he designed for great aristocrats, Bess of Hardwick's Hardwick Hall with its great expanses of glazing, or John Thynne's Longleat (left). In towns and villages across England, with wealth and peace, a great rebuilding was under way.

Much of the scientific and technological progress was related to the practical skills of navigation: English achievements in exploration were noteworthy, and these 'sea dogs' were larger-than-life characters. Sir Francis Drake circumnavigated the globe between 1577 and 1581. Martin Frobisher explored the Arctic. The first attempt at English settlement of the eastern seaboard of North America was Walter Ralegh's abortive colony at Roanoke.

Sir Francis Drake by Marcus Gheeraerts the Younger, 1591. The globe refers to Drake's circumnavigation

Tudor Life and Times
Great Tudor Palaces

Much as our own Queen Elizabeth II leaves her 'city base' of Buckingham Palace to enjoy a country weekend at Windsor, the Tudors and their vast courts travelled between their palaces. Some they used for conducting state business and hosting banquets, others mainly for their pleasure. Henry VIII was the greatest builder, creating or remodelling fabulous palaces on a massive scale, although few survive today.

The earliest measured plan of the Tower of London in 1597, showing many of its medieval and Tudor buildings still largely intact

The mighty White Tower, with its ogival turrets added by Henry VIII in 1532-3

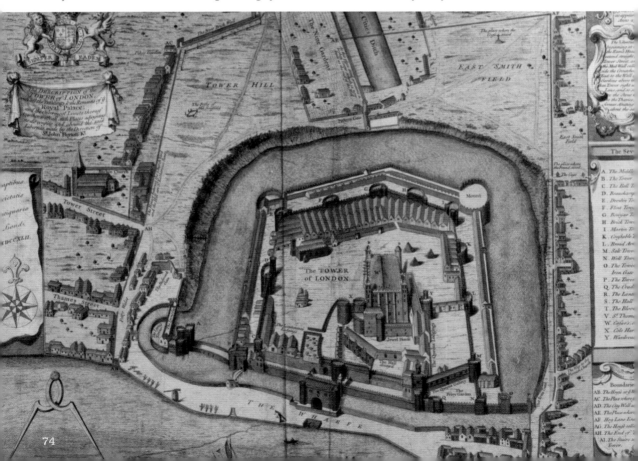

The Tower of London

When Henry VIII came to power in 1509 many aspects of the modern Tower were well established, including the royal bodyguard and among them the Yeoman Warders, a characteristic feature of the Tower today. The Tower had been only an occasional royal residence for some time and while Henry VII extended the royal lodgings, under succeeding Tudors this dwindled to nothing. Henry VIII's main gesture was to rebuild the ceremonial rooms, principally for the coronation of Anne Boleyn in 1533. It's unlikely Henry stayed at the Tower again – and Anne returned only as a prisoner for two weeks before her execution in 1536. Elizabeth was an unwilling guest in 1554, when as princess she was accused of plotting against her half-sister Queen Mary.

However, it was in the 16th century that the Tower gained its grisliest reputation as a state prison and place of execution and torture (see also page 92). Three queens, Henry VIII's second and fifth wives, Anne Boleyn and Catherine Howard, and Henry's great-niece Lady Jane Grey (queen for nine days), were held and executed at the Tower. Under Elizabeth I, the Bloody Tower was remodelled to make a comfortable lodging for Sir Walter Ralegh, who was held at the Tower for 13 years from 1603-16, then re-arrested and finally executed in 1618. The Tower played an important role in Tudor times as the nation's main arsenal, with armour, edged weapons, handguns, ordnance including heavy cannon – and most perilously, gunpowder – were all stored there under the supervision of the Office of Ordnance and the Office of Armoury.

Today's Yeoman Warders at the Tower – a detachment of the Yeoman of the Guard that have formed the royal bodyguard since Henry VIII's time

The Bloody Tower, which 'housed' high-status prisoners held at the Tower of London

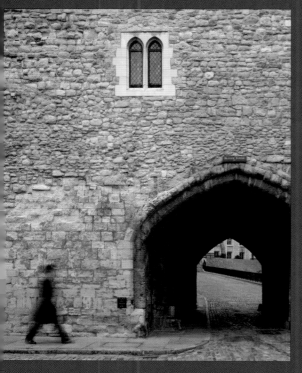

Reconstruction of Ralegh's study in the Bloody Tower, where as a high-status prisoner he lived relatively comfortably

Hampton Court Palace

Henry's VIII's most famous residence began its life as the home of Thomas Wolsey, the most powerful politician and churchman of his age. Wolsey transformed it from medieval manor to Renaissance palace and used it for ostentatious hospitality, until by 1529 his master the King wanted it for himself.

When Henry finished his own building programme in around 1540, Hampton Court was the most modern, sophisticated and magnificent palace in England. All Henry's six wives came to the palace and the architecture reflected Henry's complicated love life. Even while Henry was attempting to divorce Katherine of Aragon, work had begun on new lodgings for Katherine's rival and ultimate replacement, Anne Boleyn. She barely lived long enough to enjoy them, and when she was supplanted by Jane Seymour, Henry created a new suite of rooms on the east of the palace, along with a suite for the prince she was expected to bear. Alas, Jane died just under two weeks later from post-birth complications. Henry's children did little work to Hampton Court, but they continued to enjoy it as a country retreat.

A stained-glass window in the Great Watching Chamber, showing Cardinal Wolsey flanked by his heraldic symbols

Henry VIII by
Holbein, 1536

An illustration of Base Court, Hampton
Court Palace, from W H Pyne's *The History
of the Royal Residences*, published in 1819

The magnificent Tudor West Front, with the
Great Gatehouse, of Hampton Court Palace

St James's Palace, London

Henry built this palace on the site of St James's Hospital. Anne Boleyn spent the night after her coronation here, and the entwined initials H and A can be seen carved into a couple of the fireplaces. Henry Fitzroy, the King's illegitimate son by Bessie Blount, was living here when he died in 1536 aged 17. Much of this red-brick palace survives, including the Chapel Royal, the gatehouse and two Tudor rooms in the Royal Apartments, but it is not open to the public.

St James's Palace, from W H Pyne's *The History of the Royal Residences*, published in 1819

Windsor Castle

Henry VII made the most use of Windsor; early in his reign he held a massive feast for the Order of the Garter, and he undertook various building projects, including the construction of a three-storey tower on the west side which he used as his personal apartment.

Henry VIII enjoyed Windsor Castle as a young man, pursuing his many and varied interests: sports, wrestling, dancing, playing and writing music. During the huge northern uprising, the Pilgrimage of Grace,

Windsor was a secure southern base from which Henry managed his military response. And he was buried there. Throughout the whole Tudor period the castle also provided a sanctuary from the plagues that ravaged London. Elizabeth I spent a lot of her time at Windsor, particularly in times of crises when she knew 'it could stand a siege if need be'. It became one of her favourite locations, and she spent more money on Windsor than other properties.

Henry VIII with the Knights of the Garter, from the *Black Book of the Garter*, 1534

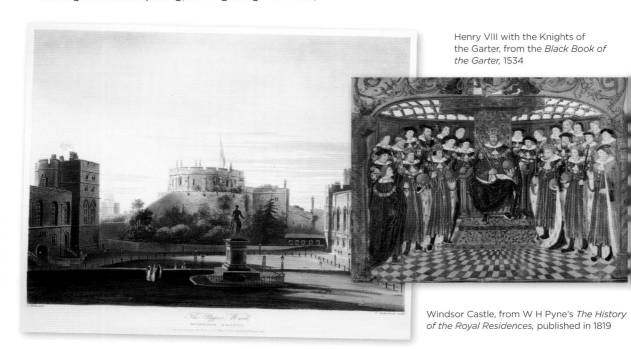

Windsor Castle, from W H Pyne's *The History of the Royal Residences,* published in 1819

Palace of Westminster

This ancient palace and abbey (most of which was destroyed in the great fire of 1834) formed the seat of Parliament, the law, royal administration and ceremonial life. The palace witnessed its last moment of royal glory in 1511: a tournament to celebrate the birth of the short-lived son of Henry and Katherine of Aragon. Royal occupancy ceased the following year when portions were gutted by fire. In 1536 the remaining parts of the old palace were absorbed into Henry's vast new Whitehall Palace (see page 80); Parliament was called upon frequently to do the King's business, not least the extraordinary programme of legislation that led to 'the break with Rome'. The royal supremacy, treason, religious conformity, the dissolution of monastic houses and the succession to Henry's throne were all issues debated and laws passed here. Parliament became an indispensable feature of government, reinforcing the position of Westminster at the heart of the nation's political life. The building we know today dates from 1834, and 'Westminster Hall' is virtually the only part of the original palace that survives.

Bird's-eye view of Whitehall Palace, which absorbed the remaining parts of the old Palace of Westminster, by Leonard Knyff, c1695

Henry VIII in Parliament, from the Wriothesley Garter book, 1523

79

The Lord Mayor's Water-Procession on the Thames, British School, 17th century, showing Whitehall Palace in the background

Tudor Life and Times
The Lost Palaces

Whitehall Palace

This magnificent palace, was built at immense cost to the personal specifications of Henry VIII incorporating York Palace. It was Cardinal Wolsey's London palace, was once the largest secular building in the country. Whitehall was conceived as a palace of two halves, separated by King Street with the river side as the royal residence for the King, his consort and courtiers in a labyrinth of rooms, chambers and courtyards. On the park side was a pleasure palace that included tennis courts, cockpits, a tiltyard and other spaces for games and amusements. The later Banqueting House excepted, this was all swept away in the great fire of 1698 and only fragments remain.

Nonsuch Palace

Nonsuch in Surrey, built in 1538, must have dazzled visitors with its mixture of timber framing, brick and stucco; painted, gilded and decorated over almost every surface. Abandoned, Nonsuch lasted until the 1680s before being sold for salvage. Archaeologists have revealed fragments of its once great riches.

Nonsuch Palace in the time of James I, Flemish School, early 17th century

Richmond Palace

Distinguished Richmond beside the Thames, once favoured by medieval kings as Sheen Palace (and renamed for Henry VII who had been Earl of Richmond), was used by Henry VIII and Katherine of Aragon in 1522 to host important Spanish visitors. Henry bestowed Richmond on Anne of Cleves after their amicable divorce. It was also the palace where Sir John Harington, Elizabeth I's godson, developed and installed England's first flushing lavatory.

Greenwich Palace

Henry VIII's (and Elizabeth's) birthplace had a special place in the King's affections. He spent a lot of time there as a young man indulging in his beloved sports and pastimes. Tennis, archery and even hand gun practice were favoured. The court enjoyed bear-baiting and cock fighting; there were kennels for the hounds and a hawk mews. An enormous new armoury was established within the grounds, while a tiltyard with viewing galleries and towers – the Tudor equivalent of a sports stadium – was built to the south.

Old Greenwich Palace, English School, 17th century

Palaces to the north of London

Pontefract Castle, West Yorkshire

During the 1541 progress, the royal party stayed at Pontefract, which must have appeared as a fairy-tale castle with its many towers and turrets. For Henry it provided only bad memories: it was here, right under his nose, that his pretty young queen Catherine Howard carried out her adulterous liaisons with Thomas Culpeper.

Hatfield Palace (now Hatfield House), Hertfordshire

Henry acquired the original palace, built by the Bishop of Ely in 1485, with the dispersal of Church possessions. Used chiefly as a residence for his three children, the house is mainly associated with Princess Elizabeth, who spend her childhood here with Edward, and later less happily under house arrest as a prisoner of her half sister Queen Mary. It was at Hatfield that Elizabeth learnt of her accession to the throne in 1558.

Pontefract Castle, by Alexander Keirincx, c1620-40

Inside a Tudor palace

A royal palace operated as a series of thresholds. To cross each closely-guarded barrier between outer public spaces to increasingly private inner chambers required progressively higher status.

An imaginary scene by the 19th-century artist Joseph Nash showing Cardinal Wolsey entertaining in the Great Watching Chamber, Hampton Court

Hampton Court is one of the few surviving palaces that demonstrate this path to prestige. What remains of the Tudor part of the palace – after Henry's apartments were demolished to make way for William and Mary's baroque masterpiece – demonstrates the size and complexity of a royal palace.

You can still see how, in royal palace style, it is designed to accommodate great numbers around the principal courtyards, yet with the focus remaining on the splendid restricted spaces at the centre, where the monarch could be found like a spider, sitting at the heart of a web.

One of the carved wooden heads known as 'Eavesdroppers' that adorn the Great Hall hammerbeam roof

Public life

Lodgings Many rooms in the palace are referred to in old records as just 'lodgings', with a cluster of this type once located around Base court. 'Lodgings' could mean anything from a simple room for a minor courtier to a magnificent suite for a visiting sovereign.

The Great Hall This magnificent space was the centre for splendid public functions and where the grandest architecture, and art, could be displayed. It was also used every day as the 'staff canteen' for the lower ranks of the Tudor Court and on special occasions, for feasting – see page 86.

Great Watching Chamber This took its name from its position as the first of the King's state apartments beyond the Great Hall, where members of the Yeomen of the Guard were stationed 'to watch' and control access through to the next sequence of more private chambers.

Above: Base Court, the first courtyard encountered by visitors to Hampton Court. The rooms off this court originally served as lodgings for courtiers and guests

Right: The east oriel window in the Great Hall, installed in the 19th century and showing Henry's lineage

Below: The Great Hall at Hampton Court, a very grand 'staff canteen' for the court and setting for splendid royal banquets

Private life

The Privy Chamber At the very centre of a Tudor palace was a fabulous 'inner realm', the Privy Chamber. The men who worked here were some of the most powerful people in the land; they enjoyed the most intimate access to the King, washing and dressing him and even attending to him on the close-stool (lavatory). His personal attendant here – the Groom of the Stool – was the most influential of all.

Access to this promised land was barred to all but the most privileged, and access to this centre of power became a goal for many an ambitious courtier. At Hampton Court (and other palaces) the galleries, libraries and gardens were out of bounds to all but a handful of trusted servants and councillors.

Withdrawing Room This (later shortened to Drawing Room) was an innovation associated with Elizabeth I. It opened off the Privy Chamber, and provided the monarch with a retreat from people who might be crowding other rooms.

Gallery This was a new type of room in the 16th century, part covered walkway for exercise and part art gallery. Henry VIII's gallery at Whitehall Palace was filled with maps in gilded frames.

Study Henry VIII's study at Eltham Palace, c1518 was furnished with coffers (oak chests), 'almoryes' (lockable cabinets) and desks with locks and keys.

King's Closet This was a small withdrawing room, forming a private space or buffer between rooms.

Bedchamber Craftsmen's bills show that Henry VIII's bed was wood panelled and gilded. When it was made every morning, and the embroidered curtains pulled back, the bed was sprinkled and blessed with holy water.

Chapel Royal Henry's chapels were magnificent and extravagant, as demonstrated by the ceiling of the Chapel Royal at Hampton Court.

Bathroom Henry had his own bathroom, in a special 'Bayne' or bath, tower, where the bathwater was heated by a fire. Other mortals had to wash themselves with cold water drawn from cisterns in the courtyards. Contamination of these was a concern; at Greenwich Palace these were painted with crosses so that 'none shall piss against them'.

The magnificent ceiling of the Chapel Royal at Hampton Court was installed for Henry VIII in 1535-6

Henry VIII reading in his bedchamber, from the *Psalter of Henry VIII*, 1540

Lavatories While lesser mortals used the communal 'jakes' or lavatories that could accommodate up to 14 men at once, Henry had his own comfortable 'close stool' or stool chamber. The King's close stools were covered with sheepskin, black velvet and silk, decorated with ribbons and provided with a burnished pewter pan in its own leather carrying case.

A rare survival of a 17th-century 'close stool' – Henry's would have been even more luxurious

Larder with a Servant, c1535-40, by Frans Snijders

Tudor pleasures and pains
Food and feasting

Life at the Tudor court may have been full of
politics and deadly intrigue, but there were
plenty of diversions for the monarch and
courtiers. Henry VIII is famous for a life lived
to the full as a younger man: feasting, hunting
for hours at a stretch, excelling at sport,
dancing and music. His son Edward had his
own pair of fighting bears, and his daughter
Elizabeth too was fond of cruel spectator
sports, bear-baiting in particular, as well as
the more poetic delights of the masque.

A 16th-century illustration of bakers making bread

The famous Tudor Kitchens at Hampton Court were built by, but not for, Henry VIII. They were magnificent, but also necessary to feed a court of 600 and show his generosity and wealth.

Food for the King The King's meals were prepared for him by his own chef in the Privy Kitchen, situated below Henry's private apartments.

On more formal occasions, dinner would be served in Henry's Presence Chamber. Then, trumpeters in livery would deliver a ceremonial fanfare as the King took his seat at a high covered table, under the canopy of state. A servant known as the 'sewer' would wash the royal hands in specially heated and scented water and dry them on a linen towel. Then on bended knee the gentlemen and ushers of his privy chamber would serve the prepared food to the King and his family.

Henry would be served around 13 dishes, and sample a little of whatever took his fancy, washing it down with choice Venetian wine, tasted first by his cup bearer. The delights set before him might include venison, game pie, pheasant, swan, heron, conger eel, lamprey (a type of fish) plus lots of delicious jellies, creams, tarts and fruit (usually cooked, as raw fruit was thought bad).

Food for the Court There were plenty of hungry people at court, but not everyone was entitled to eat at the King's expense – a privilege known as 'Bouche of Court – and not everyone received the same quality and choice of food.

The majority of the court ate in the Great Hall, with lower orders in the Kitchens themselves. The Lord Chamberlain (responsible for the running of the state rooms) drew up a list of those who were allowed two meals a day, served at 10am and 4pm, in two sittings. A daily allowance of bread, wine, beer, candles and firewood was also provided. In addition to those on the 'ordinary' rations list, there were a small number of courtiers of higher standing, who ate a better selection of food, set apart in the Great Watching Chamber.

Food for showing off For banquets and entertaining foreign visitors food became even more spectacular. Eagerly awaited parts of any banquet were the sugar and almond paste confections (occasionally wax, just for effect) known as 'subtleties'. These were moulded into fantastic sculptures, often of beasts or buildings and up to nearly a metre high, then gilded and painted.

Feasts could go on for hours. The Venetian ambassador recounted that on one occasion Henry VIII got so bored that he passed the time throwing sugarplums at his guests!

Henry in his Presence Chamber, by an unknown artist of the North-German school, early 17th century

A food historian demonstrating Tudor cookery in the Tudor Kitchens at Hampton Court Palace

Music and masque

Music and musicians constantly filled Tudor palaces, particularly at the pleasure palace of Hampton Court where dancing and masque were also key entertainments. Henry VIII himself was a talented composer and performer.

Henry playing the harp. From the *Psalter of Henry VIII*, 1540

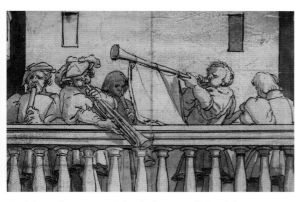

Musicians of Henry VIII, School of Hans Holbein, 16th century

New sounds The introduction of new musical instruments during this period produced a much more refined sound than had been produced during the early Middle Ages. These new musical instruments included an early form of the violin called the viol, the early oboe called the hautboy and the keyboard musical instruments called the spinet, harpsichord and the virginals.

Instruments of power Henry VIII himself owned a large collection of instruments: 26 lutes plus a collection of trumpets, viols, rebecs (medieval fiddles), sackbuts (early trombones), fifes, drums, harpsichords and organs.

Early orchestras These new musical instruments used in combination provided the Tudors with the opportunity to create unusual and creative music, a forerunner to the modern orchestra. The popularity of stringed and keyboard instruments grew tremendously during the Renaissance period.

Ambient music Henry VIII also loved a background of music. On occasions his personal organist, Dioniso Meo, also known as Dennis Memmo, would play for hours. The King employed many other musicians – by 1547 there were over 60 on the payroll, as well as singers, the Gentlemen and Children of the Chapel Royal, who followed the court from palace to palace.

Music lessons The ability to play a musical instrument was an essential skill at the courts of the great Tudor monarchs Henry VIII and Elizabeth I. Members of the royal family were taught to play musical instruments as part of their education and became skilled musicians. Henry wrote at least two sets of music for a sung mass, and the songs *Helas, madame* and *Pastime with good company* are attributed to him.

Famous legacy In 1542, the name Thomas Tallis appears in the list of Gentlemen of Henry VIII's Chapel Royal. One of the greatest composers of all time, his motet for 40 voices *Spem in alium* was probably performed for Elizabeth I's 40th birthday.

Tudor masques These festive, courtly entertainments were very popular, involving music, dancing, singing, and acting, with no expense spared on elaborate costumes and scenery. The royal family took part and women were allowed to appear; the first recorded appearance of Anne Boleyn in a masque was in 1522. Performers' faces were 'disguised' in masks, and often the King would take a leading role. Usually a masked, allegorical figure would appear and address the assembled company, providing a theme for the occasion, with musical accompaniment.

Masques at Elizabeth's court The Queen was often treated to elaborate masques put on in her honour while she was on royal progress. One particularly elaborate masque, memorably described in Sir Walter Scott's 1821 novel *Kenilworth*, was put on in 1575 at Kenilworth Castle, home of her favourite Robert Dudley, with no expense spared and naturally, it featured him in the leading role!

*Portrait of an Unknown Woman, c*1590-1600, by Marcus Gheeraerts the Younger. This lady's unusual costume suggests she was dressed for an Elizabethan or Jacobean masque

Tudor pleasures and pains
Royal sports and pastimes

A Tudor tennis ball, made of leather and hair, found at Whitehall

The young Henry VIII was sports-mad, with a passion for hunting, hawking, swordplay, tennis and other activities of pleasure and exertion. He surrounded himself with competitive young men who rode, tumbled and played as hard as he did.

Football Henry loved a good game of football, commissioning a pair of football boots at a cost of 4 shillings (about £100 today). Tudor football, in which you could pick up and throw the ball like modern day rugby, was often a violent game with no limit to the number of players. It was described as 'more of a fight than a game'. In 1540 football was banned, but young men still played in defiance of the ban and heavy fines, and large inter-village matches were popular.

Henry VIII (left) jousting at the Westminster Tournament, 1511

Real Tennis The forerunner of lawn tennis, Real Tennis was played indoors, with balls made of leather and hair. The playing of the game was similar to that of tennis today, except that the balls could also be bounced off walls. Henry VIII enjoyed the sport so much that he had courts built at many of his palaces, including Hampton Court, where he would spend huge amounts of time.

Hawking Henry spent many hours hawking, and after his death his private apartments were found to be full of falconry equipment.

Jousting This was the most prestigious sport in Tudor England. Young Henry VIII often took part in the larger competitions. He had huge tiltyards, the equivalent of modern-day sports stadiums, built at Greenwich, Whitehall and Hampton Court Palaces. As a young man Henry was fearless, and excelled at 'the tilt', but it was highly dangerous. He was nearly killed twice, and he never jousted again after a serious accident in 1536.

Hunting The young King loved to hunt all day, but in later years he avoided an arduous chase by having stags driven towards him so he could pick them off one by one. In one day's hunt in 1541 he and his courtiers shot 200 deer.

Bear baiting and cock fighting Both Henry and Elizabeth attended these barbaric events. Elizabeth particularly enjoyed seeing bear baiting and when she toured on royal progress, towns would put on big displays for her. There was a ring built at Whitehall Palace so that Tudor kings and queens could watch from a window in comfort. In 1585 a member of parliament tried to ban bear baiting, but Elizabeth overruled him.

Bowls This was one of the gentler sports of Tudor England. Some of the nobility developed lawns for the sole purpose of playing the sport.

Cards and board games were also extremely popular, with games such as Trump being invented during Tudor times. It is said that Queen Elizabeth used to cheat mercilessly at card games and always played to win!

Tudor pains
Torture and execution

The seemingly bloodthirsty and vengeful nature of the Tudor regime is nowhere better illustrated than in its use of execution and torture as instruments of justice. Treason laws were extended, and deaths were often cruel.

Before he made a daring escape from the Tower of London in 1597, the Jesuit priest Father John Gerard was tortured to try to confess to plotting against the life of Queen Elizabeth, He described his ordeal: with his arms held in iron rings,

> ... they left me hanging by my hands and arms fastened above my head... Hanging like this I began to pray. The gentlemen standing around me asked me whether I was willing to confess now. 'I cannot and I will not,' I answered.

After the agony and falling unconscious, he was eventually taken down.

In the course of the 16th century, many hundreds were executed, and a smaller number – but not an insignificant one – underwent torture, as Gerard did. Torture, although used sparingly, was designed to elicit information. The rack, manacles, compression devices such as the 'scavenger's daughter', were all brought into play. For many prisoners just being shown the instruments of torture was enough to persuade them to talk. Others were made of hardier material.

Treason laws were extended a number of times. Henry VIII in particular, but also his daughters, used execution as a means to enforce conformity and smother dissent. Execution was also a primary penalty for a great range of other crimes and misdeeds.

The usual method was hanging. Traitors often suffered hanging, drawing and quartering, when they were drawn on hurdles to the place of execution, commonly at Tyburn; there they were hanged by the neck for a while, pulled down from the scaffold, their internal organs taken out while they were still alive, and then their bodies were chopped into four parts. Religious heretics and suspected witches were often burned, at Smithfield or in provincial cities. Some, like Margaret Clitheroe, were crushed to death. Beheading with an axe was usually reserved for important traitors, such as Thomas More and Thomas Cromwell, on Tower Hill, or like Henry VIII's two executed queens within the Tower of London itself.

In the early years of Henry VIII's reign, executions were used to prevent Protestant ideas coming in; after 1536 they were used to help promote the Reformation and ensure conformity. The reign of Mary witnessed a rage of executions of Protestants. In the reign of Elizabeth judicial anger was turned onto Catholics, especially after the Queen had been excommunicated by the Pope and priests like Gerard were sent to England to bring the country back to Catholicism and to plot the Queen's overthrow or murder.

The scale and ferocity of judicial murder in the Tudor period was probably unequalled in English history.

The torture of the Jesuit priest, Father John Gerard at the Tower of London

The legacy of the Tudors

The Tudors have left a powerful legacy that reaches into many aspects of our lives and national psyche, even though they lived four or five hundred years ago.

- Henry VIII – the most immediately recognisable monarch in British history.

- William Shakespeare – the greatest English dramatist of the Tudor or any other era.

- The Bible in English.

- The Church of England, with the monarch as its head.

- Exploration, colonisation and trading companies in North and South America, Asia and Africa.

- Parliament, established as an integral and necessary part of political life and decision-making.

- A small and peripheral island nation becoming a major European power.

- Women being accepted as monarchs in their own right.

- Great architecture, from King's College Chapel to Hampton Court Palace to Hardwick Hall.

- The central importance of London

- Union with Scotland, that came with the succession of James VI of Scotland as James I of England in 1603 after Elizabeth I died without a direct heir.

- Parish registers, introduced by Thomas Cromwell in 1537.

Acknowledgements

Published by Historic Royal Palaces
Hampton Court Palace
Surrey
KT8 9AU

© Historic Royal Palaces 2015

ISBN 978-1-873993-34-7

Written by Sarah Kilby and David Souden

Edited by Sarah Kilby
Picture research by Susan Mennell
Designed by Brand Remedy
Printed by BKT

 Find us on Facebook: **Historic Royal Palaces**

Follow us on Twitter **@HRP_palaces**

Watch us on You Tube
www.youtube.com/HistoricRoyalPalaces

Historic Royal Palaces

Historic Royal Palaces is the charity that looks after:

Tower of London
Hampton Court Palace
Banqueting House
Kensington Palace
Kew Palace
Hillsborough Castle

We help everyone explore the story of how monarchs and people have shaped society, in some of the greatest palaces ever built

We raise all our own funds and depend on the support of our visitors, members, donors, sponsors and volunteers.

For images owned by Historic Royal Palaces, please visit our online image library at **www.images.hrp.org.uk**

Cover illustrations

(1) Mary I (Bridgeman Images/Prado, Madrid, Spain),
(2) Edward VI (© National Portrait Gallery, London),
(3) Henry VIII (Bridgeman Images/Burghley House Collection, Lincolnshire, UK),
(4) Elizabeth I (© National Portrait Gallery, London)
(5) Henry VII (Royal Collection Trust/© Her Majesty Queen Elizabeth II 2015)

Main illustrations

Abbreviations: b = bottom, c = centre, l = left, r = right, t = top

Reproduced by kind permission of His Grace, The Duke of Bedford and the Trustees of the Bedford Estates: page 52t; From the collection at Blair Castle, Perthshire: page 17; Bodleian Library, University of Oxford: page 86b (Ms Canon Liturg 99 fol 16); Bridgeman Images: pages 5b (Sudeley Castle, Winchcombe, Gloucestershire, UK), 13tl (National Library, St. Petersburg, Russia), 15 (Forbes Magazine Collection, New York, USA), 19 (private collection), 23 (Kunsthistoriches Museum, Vienna, Austria), 25 (Louvre, Paris, France), 27 (private collection), 31c (Corpus Christi College, Oxford, UK), 33b (Galleria degli Uffizi, Florence, Italy), 39 (private collection), 41l (National Gallery of Washington DC, USA), 41r (private collection), 42 (National Portrait Gallery, London, UK), 43 (Society of Antiquaries, London), 44tr (Hoberman/UIG), 45 (Weston Park Foundation, UK), 46 (private collection), 48 (private collection), 53 (Prado, Madrid, Spain), 62t (Hatfield House, Hertfordshire, UK), 70t (private collection), 72-73 (private collection/© Arthur Ackermann Ltd., London), 77tl (Thyssen-Bornemisza Collection, Madrid, Spain), 80b (Fitzwilliam Museum, University of Cambridge, UK), 81t (Wakefield Museums and Galleries, West Yorkshire, UK), 81b (National Trust Photographic Library/Kingston Lacy, Dorset, UK), 86t (Mead Art Museum, Amherst College, MA, USA); © The British Library Board: pages 12, 14t, 85t, 88; © The Trustees of the British Museum: pages 87l, 89t; The College of Arms: pages 40-41, 90-91; © The Dean and Canons of Windsor: page 78br; Harley Gallery: page 61; © Historic Royal Palaces: 2-3, 5tr, 6, 8, 13bl, 13r, 14b, 27 (inset), 74t, 74b, 75t, 75bl, 75br, 76-77, 76t, 77tr, 78t, 78bl, 82t, 82b, 83t, 83bl, 83br, 84, 87r, 90t; London Metropolitan Archives (with kind permission of the Worshipful Company of Plaisterers, incorporated by Royal Charter 1501): page 7; Courtesy of the Museum of London: page 38; © Copyright The National Gallery, London 2015: page 49; © National Maritime Museum, Greenwich, London: pages 68-69, 73; © National Museums Liverpool (The Walker Art Gallery): page 95; © National Portrait Gallery, London: pages 5tl, 11, 21, 28, 30b, 31t, 31b, 35, 47, 50, 51t, 52b, 54, 57r, 58, 62b, 63t, 63b, 65t; © National Trust Images: page 34 (Derrick E. Witty); Royal Collection Trust/© Her Majesty Queen Elizabeth II 2015: pages 5tc, 9, 10, 16l, 16r, 30t, 32, 33t, 60, 67, 79b, 80t, 85b, 89b; Topfoto: pages 36 (Bridgeman Images), 37 (©Fotomas), 44bl (The Granger Collection), 44br (Bridgeman Images), 51b (The Granger Collection), 56t (World History Archive), 56b (The Granger Collection), 57l (The Granger Collection), 70b (The Granger Collection), 71 (© The British Library Board), 93 (© The British Library Board); © The Victoria and Albert Museum, London: page 65b; © By kind permission of the Trustees of the Wallace Collection, London: page 64; Westminster City Archives: page 79t.

Historic Royal Palaces is a registered charity (no. 1068852)

www.hrp.org.uk